The Wisdom of
THE KORAN

Also available from The Wisdom Library

THE WISDOM OF GANDHI
THE WISDOM OF GIBRAN
THE WISDOM OF THE KABBALAH
THE WISDOM OF THE KORAN
THE WISDOM OF MUHAMMAD
THE WISDOM OF SARTRE
THE WISDOM OF THE TALMUD
THE WISDOM OF THOREAU

Published by Citadel Press

The Wisdom of
THE KORAN

PHILOSOPHICAL
LIBRARY

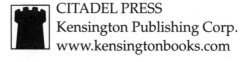

CITADEL PRESS
Kensington Publishing Corp.
www.kensingtonbooks.com

The present selection is taken from the work *The Qur'an* translated by E. H. Palmer of St. John College, Cambridge, 1880.

CITADEL PRESS books are published by Kensington Publishing Corp., 850 Third Avenue, New York, NY 10022. Citadel Press and its logo are trademarks of Kensington Publishing Corp.

Titles included in the Wisdom Library are published by arrangement with Philosophical Library.

All Kensington titles, imprints, and distributed lines are available at special quantity discounts for bulk purchases for sales promotions, premiums, fund raising, educational, or institutional use. Special book excerpts or customized printings can also be created to fit specific needs. For details, write or phone the office of the Kensington special sales manager: Kensington Publishing Corp., 850 Third Avenue, New York, NY 10022, attn: Special Sales Department, phone 1-800-221-2647.

First Wisdom Library printing May 2001

10 9 8 7 6 5 4 3 2 1

Printed in the United States of America

Cataloging data for *The Wisdom of the Koran* may be obtained from the Library of Congress.

ISBN 0-8065-2253-4

The Koran, or The Book, is the basis of Islamic religion. Most of it was written by Mohammed Ibn-Abdallah (570–632), who, while adapting many of the Judaic and Christian teachings, endeavored to restore what he considered the true Faith of Abraham. While Mohammed strongly felt that he was the one and only prophet of Allah, he rejected personal cult as well as the performing of miracles.

Salvation must come through the great prophets from Moses to Mohammed. The Koran is a guide for the pious who perform not only ritual duties but also excel in charity. Theirs is also the final reward on Judgment Day. The impact of the Koran upon the Moslem world was immense upon the social and personal life of all its adherents.

CONTENTS

The Wisdom of
THE KORAN

The Chapter of the Night Journey[1].

In the name of the merciful and compassionate God.

Celebrated be the praises of Him who took His servant a journey by night from the Sacred Mosque[2] to the Remote Mosque[3], the precinct of which we have blessed, to show him of our signs! verily, He both hears and looks.

And we gave Moses the Book and made it a guidance to the children of Israel: 'Take ye to no guardian but me.'

Seed of those we bore with Noah (in the ark)! verily, he was a thankful servant!

And we decreed to the children of Israel in the Book, 'Ye shall verily do evil in the earth twice[4], and ye shall rise to a great height (of pride).'

---

[1] Also called 'The Children of Israel.' The subject of Mohammed's miraculous journey in one night from Mecca to Jerusalem, and his ascent into heaven, will be found discussed in the Introduction.

[2] The Kaabah at Mecca.

[3] The Temple at Jerusalem.

[4] The Mohammedan commentators interpret this as referring the first to either Goliath, Sennacherib, or Nebuchadnezzar, and the latter to a sec-

[5] And when the threat for the first (sin) of the two came, we sent over them servants of ours, endued with violence, and they searched inside your houses; and it was an accomplished threat.

Then we rallied you once more against them, and aided you with wealth and sons, and made you a numerous band.

'If ye do well, ye will do well to your own souls; and if ye do ill, it is against them!

'And when the threat for the last came[1]—to harm your faces and to enter the mosque as they entered it the first time, and to destroy what they had got the upper-hand over with utter destruction.'

It may be that thy Lord will have mercy on you;—but if ye return we will return, and we have made hell a prison for the misbelievers.

Verily, this Qur'ân guides to the straightest path, and gives the glad tidings to the believers [10] who do aright that for them is a great hire; and that for those who believe not in the hereafter, we have prepared a mighty woe.

Man prays for evil as he prays for good; and man was ever hasty.

We made the night and the day two signs; and we blot out the sign of the night and make the sign of the day visible, that ye may seek after plenty from your Lord, and that ye may number the years and the reckoning; and we have detailed everything in detail.

And every man's augury[2] have we fastened on his neck;

ond Persian invasion. The two sins committed by the Jews, and for which these punishments were threatened and executed, were, first, the murder of Isaiah and the imprisonment of Jeremiah, and the second, the murder of John the Baptist. Mohammedan views of ancient history are, however, vague.

[1] Supply, 'we sent foes.'

[2] I.e. 'fortune' or 'fate,' literally, 'bird;' the Arabs, like the ancient Romans, having been used to practise divination from the flight of birds.

and we will bring forth for him on the resurrection day a book offered to him wide open. [15] 'Read thy book, thou art accountant enough against thyself to-day!'

He who accepts guidance, accepts it only for his own soul: and he who errs, errs only against it; nor shall one burdened soul bear the burden of another.

Nor would we punish until we had sent an apostle. And when we desired to destroy a city we bade[1] the opulent ones thereof; and they wrought abomination therein; and its due sentence was pronounced; and we destroyed it with utter destruction.

How many generations have we destroyed after Noah! but thy Lord of the sins of his servant is well aware, and sees enough.

Whoso is desirous of this life that hastens away, we will hasten on for him therein what we please,—for whom we please. Then we will make hell for him to broil in—despised and outcast.

[20] But whoso desires the next life, and strives for it and is a believer—these, their striving shall be gratefully received.

To all—these and those—will we extend the gifts of thy Lord; for the gifts of thy Lord are not restricted.

See how we have preferred some of them over others, but in the next life are greater degrees and greater preference.

Put not with God other gods, or thou wilt sit despised and forsaken.

Thy Lord has decreed that ye shall not serve other than Him; and kindness to one's parents, whether one or both of them reach old age with thee; and say not to them, 'Fie!' and do not grumble at them, but speak to them a generous speech. [25] And lower to them the wing of humility out of

---

[1] Bade them obey the Apostle.

compassion, and say, 'O Lord! have compassion on them as they brought me up when I was little!' Your Lord knows best what is in your souls if ye be righteous, and, verily, He is forgiving unto those who come back penitent.

And give thy kinsman his due and the poor and the son of the road; and waste not wastefully, for the wasteful were ever the devil's brothers; and the devil is ever ungrateful to his Lord.

[30] But if thou dost turn away from them to seek after mercy from thy Lord[1], which thou hopest for, then speak to them an easy speech.

Make not thy hand fettered to thy neck, nor yet spread it out quite open, lest thou shouldst have to sit down blamed and straitened in means. Verily, thy Lord spreads out provision to whomsoever He will or He doles it out. Verily, He is ever well aware of and sees His servants.

And slay not your children for fear of poverty; we will provide for them; beware! for to slay them is ever a great sin!

And draw not near to fornication; verily, it is ever an abomination, and evil is the way thereof.

[35] And slay not the soul that God has forbidden you, except for just cause; for he who is slain unjustly we have given his next of kin authority; yet let him not exceed in slaying; verily, he is ever helped.

And draw not near to the wealth of the orphan, save to improve it, until he reaches the age of puberty, and fulfil your compacts; verily, a compact is ever enquired of.

And give full measure when ye measure out, and weigh with a right balance; that is better and a fairer determination.

---

[1] I.e. if you are compelled to leave them in order to seek your livelihood; or if your present means are insufficient to enable you to relieve others.

And do not pursue that of which thou hast no knowledge; verily, the hearing, the sight, and the heart, all of these shall be enquired of.

And walk not on the earth proudly; verily, thou canst not cleave the earth, and thou shalt not reach the mountains in height.

[40] All this is ever evil in the sight of your Lord and abhorred.

That is something of what thy Lord has inspired thee with of wisdom; do not then put with God other gods, or thou wilt be thrown into hell reproached and outcast. What! has your Lord chosen to give you sons, and shall He take for Himself females among the angels? verily, ye are speaking a mighty speech.

Now have we turned it in various ways in this Qur'ân, so let them bear in mind; but it will only increase them in aversion.

Say, 'Were there with Him other gods, as ye say, then would they seek a way against the Lord of the throne.'

[45] Celebrated be His praises, and exalted be He above what they say with great exaltation!

The seven heavens and the earth celebrate His praises, and all who therein are; nor is their aught but what celebrates His praise: but ye cannot understand their celebration;—verily, He is clement and forgiving.

And when thou readest the Qur'ân we place between thee and those who believe not in the hereafter a covering veil. And we place covers upon their hearts, lest they should understand, and dulness in their ears.

And when thou dost mention in the Qur'ân thy Lord by Himself they turn their backs in aversion.

[50] We know best for what they listen when they listen to thee; and when they whisper apart—when the wrongdoers say, 'Ye only follow a man enchanted.'

Behold, how they strike out for you parables, and err, and cannot find the way!

They say, 'What! when we have become bones and rubbish are we to be raised up a new creature?' Say, 'Be ye stones, or iron, or a creature, the greatest your breasts can conceive—!' Then they shall say, 'Who is to restore us?' Say, 'He who originated you at first;' and they will wag their heads and say, 'When will that be?' Say, 'It may, perhaps, be nigh.'

The day when He shall call on you and ye shall answer with praise to Him, and they will think that they have tarried but a little.

[55] And say to my servants that they speak in a kind way[1]; verily, Satan makes ill-will between them; verily, Satan was ever unto man an open foe.

Your Lord knows you best; if He please He will have mercy upon you, or if He please He will torment you: but we have not sent thee to take charge of them.

And thy Lord best knows who is in the heavens and the earth; we did prefer some of the prophets over the others, and to David did we give the Psalms.

Say, 'Call on those whom ye pretend other than God;' but they shall not have the power to remove distress from you, nor to turn if off.

Those on whom they call[2], seek themselves for a means of approaching their Lord, (to see) which of them is nearest:

[1] I.e. they are not to provoke the idolaters by speaking too roughly to them so as to exasperate them.

[2] Sale interprets this to mean 'the angels and prophets.' Rodwell remarks that it is an 'obvious allusion to the saint worship of the Christians.' As, however, precisely the same expression is used elsewhere in the Qur'ân for the false gods of the Arabs, and the existence of those ginns and angels whom they associated with God is constantly recognised, their divinity only being denied, I prefer to follow the Moslem commentators, and refer the passage to the gods of the Arabian pantheon at Mecca; cf. Part I, p. 127, note 2.

and they hope for His mercy and they fear His torment; verily, the torment of thy Lord is a thing to beware of.

[60] There is no city but we will destroy it before the day of judgment, or torment it with keen torment;—that is in the Book inscribed.

Naught hindered us from sending thee with signs, save that those of yore said they were lies; so we gave Thamûd the visible she-camel, but they treated her unjustly! for we do not send (any one) with signs save to make men fear.

And when we said to thee, 'Verily, thy Lord encompasses men!' and we made the vision which we showed thee only a cause of sedition unto men, and the cursed tree[1] as well; for we will frighten them, but it will only increase them in great rebellion.

And when we say to the angels, 'Adore Adam;' and they adored, save Iblîs, who said, 'Am I to adore one whom Thou hast created out of clay?'

Said he, 'Dost thou see now? this one whom Thou hast honoured above me, verily, if Thou shouldst respite me until the resurrection day, I will of a surety utterly destroy his seed except a few.'

[65] Said He, 'Begone! and whoso of them follows thee—verily, hell is your recompense, and ample recompense. Entice away whomsoever of them thou canst with thy voice; and bear down upon them with thy horse and with thy foot; and share with them in the wealth and their children; and promise them,—but Satan promises them naught but deceit. Verily, my servants, thou hast no authority over them; thy Lord is guardian enough over them!'

---

[1] The Zaqqûm; see Chapter XXXVII, verse 60. The vision referred to is the night journey to heaven, although those commentators who believe this to have been an actual fact suppose another vision to account for this passage.

It is your Lord who drives the ships for you in the sea that ye may seek after plenty from Him; verily, He is ever merciful to you. And when distress touches you in the sea, those whom ye call on, except Him, stray away from you; but when He has brought you safe to shore, ye turn away; for man is ever ungrateful.

[70] Are ye sure that He will not cleave with you the side of the shore, or send against you a heavy sand-storm? then ye will find no guardian for yourselves.

Or are ye sure that He will not send you back therein another time, and send against you a violent wind, and drown you for your misbelief? then ye will find for yourselves no protector against us.

But we have been gracious to the children of Adam, and we have borne them by land and sea, and have provided them with good things, and have preferred them over many that we have created.

The day when we will call all men by their high priest; and he whose book is given in his right hand—these shall read their book, nor shall they be wronged a straw. But he who in this life is blind shall be blind in the next too, and err farther from the way.

[75] They had well-nigh beguiled thee from what we inspired thee with, that thou shouldst forge against us something else, and then they would have taken thee for a friend; and had it not been that we stablished thee, thou wouldst have well-nigh leant towards them a little: then would we have made thee taste of torment both of life and death, then thou wouldst not have found against us any helper[1].

---

[1] The commentators say that this refers to a treaty proposed by the tribe of THaqîf, who insisted, as a condition of their submission, that they should be exempt from the more irksome duties of Muslims, and should be allowed to retain their idol Allât for a certain time, and that their territory should be considered sacred, like that of Mecca.

And they well-nigh enticed thee away from the land, to turn thee out therefrom; but then—they should not have tarried after thee except a little.

[This is] the course of those of our prophets whom we have sent before thee; and thou shalt find no change in our course.

[80] Be thou steadfast in prayer from the declining of the sun until the dusk of the night, and the reading of the dawn; verily, the reading of the dawn is ever testified to.

And for the night, watch thou therein as an extra service. It may be that thy Lord will raise thee to a laudable station.

And say, 'O my Lord! make me enter with a just entry; and make me come forth with a just coming forth; and grant me from Thee authority to aid.'

And say, 'Truth has come, and falsehood has vanished! verily, falsehood is transient.'

And we will send down of the Qur'ân that which is a healing and a mercy to the believers, but it will only increase the wrong-doers in loss.

[85] And when we favour man he turns away and retires aside, but when evil touches him he is ever in despair. Say, 'Every one acts after his own manner, but your Lord knows best who is most guided in the way.'

They will ask thee of the spirit[1]. Say, 'The spirit comes at the bidding of my Lord, and ye are given but a little knowledge thereof.'

If we had wished we would have taken away that with which we have inspired thee; then thou wouldst have found no guardian against us, unless by a mercy from thy Lord; verily, His grace towards thee is great!

[90] Say, 'If mankind and ginns united together to bring

---

[1] According to some, the soul generally; but according to others, and more probably, the angel Gabriel as the agent of revelation.

the like of this Qur'ân, they could not bring the like, though they should back each other up!'

We have turned about for men in this Qur'ân every parable; but most men refuse to accept it, save ungratefully.

And they say, 'We will by no means believe in thee, until there gush forth for thee a fountain from the earth; or there be made for thee a garden of palms and grapes, and rivers come gushing out admist them; or thou make the sky to fall down upon us in pieces; or thou bring us God and the angels before us; [95] or there be made for thee a house of gold; or thou climb up into the heaven; and even then we will not believe in thy climbing there, until thou send down on us a book that we may read!'

Say, 'Celebrated be the praises of my Lord! was I aught but a mortal apostle?'

Naught prohibited men from believing when the guidance came to them, save their saying, 'God has sent a mortal for an apostle.'

Say, 'Were there angels on the earth walking in quiet, we had surely sent them an angel as an apostle.'

Say, 'God is witness enough between me and you; verily, He is ever of His servants well aware, and sees.'

He whom God guides, he is guided indeed; and he whom God leads astray, thou shalt never find patrons for them beside Him; and we will gather them upon the resurrection day upon their faces, blind, and dumb, and deaf; their resort is hell; whenever it grows dull we will give them another blaze!

[100] That is their reward for that they disbelieved in our signs, and said, 'What! when we are bones and rubbish, shall we then be raised up a new creation?'

Could they not see that God who created the heavens and the earth is able to create the like of them, and to set for them an appointed time; there is no doubt therein, yet the wrong-doers refuse to accept it, save ungratefully!

Say, 'Did ye control the treasuries of the mercy of my Lord, then ye would hold them through fear of expending; for man is ever niggardly!'

And we did bring Moses nine manifest signs; then ask the children of Israel (about) when he came to them, and Pharaoh said to him, 'Verily, I think thee, O Moses! enchanted.'

He said, 'Well didst thou know that none sent down these save the Lord of the heavens and the earth as visible signs; and, verily, I think thee, O Pharaoh! ruined.'

[105] And he desired to drive them out of the land; but we drowned him and those with him, one and all.

And after him we said to the children of Israel, 'Dwell ye in the land; and when the promise of the hereafter comes to pass, we will bring you in a mixed crowd (to judgment).

'In truth have we sent it down, and in truth has it come down; and we have not sent thee as aught but a herald of glad tidings and a warner.

'And a Qur'ân which we have divided, that thou mayst read it to mankind leisurely, and we sent it down, sending it down[1].'

Say, 'Believe ye therein, or believe not; verily, those who were given the knowledge before it, when it is read to them fall down upon their beards adoring! and they say, "Celebrated be the praises of our Lord! verily, the promise of our Lord is ever fulfilled"—they fall down upon their beards weeping, and it increases their humility.'

[110] Say, 'Call on God, or call on the Merciful One, whichever ye may call on Him by; for His are the best of names[1].'

---

[1] As occasion required.

And do not say thy prayers openly, nor yet murmur them, but seek a way between these.

And say, 'Praise belongs to God, who has not taken to Himself a son, and has not had a partner in His kingdom, nor had a patron against (such) abasement.' And magnify Him greatly[2]!

---

[1] The Arabs whom Mohammed addressed seem to have imagined that he meant by Allâh and Ar-ra'hmân (the Merciful One) two separate deities. The various epithets which are applied to God in the Qur'ân, such as 'kind,' 'seeing,' 'knowing,' &c., are called by the Muslims al'as-mâ'u'l'husnâ, 'the best of names,' and are repeated in telling the beads of their rosary.

[2] This command is obeyed by the Muslims frequently pronouncing the phrase Allâhu akbar, especially as an expression of astonishment. It is the same expression as that used by the Egyptian women concerning Joseph.

The Chapter of the Cave.

In the name of the merciful and compassionate God.

Praise belongs to God, who sent down to His servant the Book, and put no crookedness therein,—straight, to give warning of keen violence from Him; and to give the glad tidings to the believers, who do what is right, that for them is a goodly reward wherein they shall abide for ever and for aye; and to give warning to those who say, 'God hath taken to Himself a son.'

They have no knowledge thereof, nor their fathers; a serious word it is that comes forth from their mouths! verily, they only speak a lie!

[5] Haply thou wilt grieve thyself to death for sorrow after them, if they believe not in this new revelation. Verily, we have made what is on the earth an ornament thereof, to try them, which of them is best in works; but verily, we are going to make what is thereon bare soil.

Hast thou reckoned that the Fellows of the Cave and Er-raqîm were a wonder amongst our signs[1]?'

When the youths resorted to the cave and said, 'O our Lord! bring us mercy from Thee, and dispose for us our affair aright!'

[10] And we struck their ears (with deafness) in the cave

---

[1] This is the well-known story of the Seven Sleepers of Ephesus. What is meant by Er-raqîm no one knows. The most generally accepted Mohammedan theory is that it was a dog belonging to the party; though some commentators take it to be the name of the valley or mountain in which the cave was situated; others again say that it was a metal plate inscribed with the name of the Sleepers.

for a number of years. Then we raised them up again, that we might know which of the two crews[1] could best calculate the time of their tarrying. We will narrate to thee their story in truth. Verily, they were youths who believed in their Lord, and we added to their guidance, and we braced up their hearts, when they stood up and said, 'Our Lord is the Lord of the heavens and the earth, we will not call upon any god beside Him, for then we should have said an extravagant thing. These people of ours have taken to other gods beside Him. Though they do not bring any manifest authority for them. And who is more unjust than he who forges against God a lie?

[15] 'So when ye have gone apart from them and what they serve other than God, then resort ye to the cave. Our Lord will unfold His mercy to you, and will dispose for you your affair advantageously.'

And thou mightst have seen the sun when it rose decline from their cave towards the right hand, and when it set leave them on the left hand, while they were in the spacious part thereof. That is one of the signs of God. Whom God guides he is guided indeed, and whom He leads astray thou shalt surely find for him no patron to guide aright. Thou mightst have reckoned them waking though they were sleeping, as we turned them towards the right and towards the left; and their dog spreading out his fore-paws on the threshold. Hadst thou come suddenly upon them thou wouldst surely have turned and fled away from them, and wouldst surely have been filled by them with dread.

Thus did we raise them up that they might question each other. Spake a speaker amongst them, 'How long have ye

---

[1] That is, the youths themselves or the people they met on their awakening.

tarried?' They said, 'We have tarried a day or part of a day.'
They said, 'Your Lord knows best your tarrying; so send
one of you with this coin of yours to the city, and let him
look which of them has the purest food, and let him bring
you provision thereof; and let him be subtle and not let any
one perceive you. Verily, they—should they perceive you—
would stone you, or would force you back again unto their
faith, and ye would never prosper then.'

[20] Thus did we make their people acquainted with
their story, that they might know that God's promise is true;
and that the Hour, there is no doubt concerning it. When
they disputed amongst themselves concerning their affair,
and said, 'Build a building over them, their Lord knows
best about them;' and those who prevailed in their affair
said, 'We will surely make a mosque over them.'

They will say, 'Three, and the fourth of them was their
dog:' and they will say, 'Five, and the sixth of them was
their dog:' guessing at the unseen: and they will say, 'Seven,
and the eighth of them was their dog.' Say, 'My Lord knows
best the number of them; none knows them but a few.'

Dispute not therefore concerning them save with a
plain disputation, and ask not any one of them[1] concerning them.

And never say of anything, 'Verily, I am going to do that
to-morrow,' except 'if God please;' and remember thy Lord
when thou hast forgotten, and say, 'It may be that my Lord
will guide me to what is nearer to the right than this[2].'

They tarried in their cave three hundred years and nine
more. [25] Say, 'God knows best of their tarrying. His are

---

[1] That is, the Christians.

[2] Mohammed, being asked by the Jews concerning the number of the
Seven Sleepers, had promised to bring them a revelation upon the subject
on the morrow: this verse is a rebuke for his presumption.

the unseen things of the heavens and the earth—He can see! and hear[1]!'

They have no patron beside Him, nor does He let any one share in His judgment. So, recite what thou art inspired with of the Book of thy Lord; there is no changing His words; nor shalt thou ever find a refuge beside Him; and keep thyself patient, with those who call upon their Lord morning and evening, desiring His face; nor let thine eyes be turned from them, desiring the adornment of the life of this world; and obey not him[2] whose heart we have made heedless of remembrance of us, and who follows his lusts, for his affair is ever in advance (of the truth).

But say, 'The truth is from your Lord, so let him who will, believe; and let him who will, disbelieve.' Verily, we have prepared for the evildoers a fire, sheets of which shall encompass them; and if they cry for help, they shall be helped with water like molten brass, which shall roast their faces:—an ill drink and an evil couch!

Verily, those who believe and act aright,—verily, we will not waste the hire of him who does good works.

[30] These, for them are gardens of Eden; beneath them rivers flow; they shall be adorned therein with bracelets of gold, and shall wear green robes of silk, and of brocade; reclining therein on thrones;—pleasant is the reward, and goodly the couch!

[1] This expression Sale takes to be ironical, and translates, 'make thou him to see and hear;' Rodwell renders it, 'look thou and hearken unto him:' both translators having missed both the force of the idiom and the explanation given by the commentators Al Bâidhâvî and Jalâlâin, to whom Sale refers. The meaning is that which I have given, and the idiom is equivalent to that which occurs in a passage of Harîrî, Maqâmah 3 (p. 30, De Sacy's first edition), a krim bihi, 'how noble it is!' abzar bihi being equivalent to mâ abzarahu, 'how observant He is!'

[2] Said to refer to Ommâiyet ibn 'Half, who had requested Mohammed to give up his poorer followers to please the Qurâis.

Strike out for them a parable: Two men, for one of whom we made two gardens of grapes, and surrounded them with palms, and put corn between the two. Each of the two gardens brought forth its food and did not fail in aught. And we caused a river to gush forth admidst them; and he had fruit, and said unto his fellow, who was his next-door neighbour, 'I am more wealthy than thee, and mightier of household.'

And he went unto his garden, having wronged himself: said he, 'I do not think that this will ever disappear; and I do not think that the hour is imminent; and if even I be sent back unto my Lord, I shall find a better one than it in exchange.'

[35] Said unto him his fellow, who was his next-door neighbour, 'Thou hast disbelieved in Him who created thee from earth, and then from a clot, then fashioned thee a man; but God, He is my Lord; nor will I associate any one with my Lord. Why couldst thou not have said, when thou didst go into thy garden, "What God pleases[1]! there is no power save in God,"—to look at, I am less than thee in wealth and children; but haply my Lord will give me something better than thy garden, and will send upon it thunder-claps from the sky, and it shall be on the morrow bare slippery soil; or on the morrow its water may be deeply sunk, so that thou canst not get thereat!'

[40] And his fruits were encompassed, and on the morrow he turned down the palms of his hands[2] for what he had spent thereon, for it was fallen down upon its trellises. And he said, 'Would that I had never associated any one with my Lord!' And he had not any party to help him be-

---

[1] In the original Mâ sâ allâh; this is the usual formula for expressing admiration among Muslims.

[2] I.e. wrung his hands.

side God, nor was he helped. In such a case the patronage is God's, the true; He is best at rewarding and best at bringing to an issue.

Strike out for them, too, a parable of the life of this world; like water which we send down from the sky, and the vegetation of the earth is mingled therewith;—and on the morrow it is dried up, and the winds scatter it; for God is powerful over all.

Wealth and children are an adornment of the life of this world; but enduring good works are better with thy Lord, as a recompense, and better as a hope.

[45] And the day when we will move the mountains, and thou shalt see the (whole) earth stalking forth; and we will gather them, and will not leave one of them behind. Then shall they be presented to thy Lord in ranks.—Now have ye come to us as we created you at first! nay, but ye thought that we would never make our promise good!

And the Book shall be placed[1], and thou shalt see the sinners in fear of what is in it; and they will say, 'Alas, for us! what ails this Book, it leaves neither small nor great things alone, without numbering them?' and they shall find present what they have done; and thy Lord will not wrong any one.

And when we said to the angels, 'Adore Adam,' they adored him, save only Iblîs, who was of the ginn, who revolted from the bidding of his Lord. 'What! will ye then take him and his seed as patrons, rather than me, when they are foes of yours? bad for the wrong-doers is the exchange!'

I did not make them witnesses of the creation of the heavens and the earth, nor of the creation of themselves, nor did I take those who lead astray for my supporters.

[1] In the hand of each.

[50] On the day when He shall say, 'Call ye my partners whom ye pretend:' and they shall call on them, but they shall not answer them; and we will set the vale of perdition between them; and the sinners shall see the fire, and shall think that they are going to fall therein, and shall find no escape therefrom. We have turned about in this Qur'ân for men every parable; but man is ever at most things a caviller.

Naught prevented men from believing when the guidance came to them, or from asking pardon of their Lord, except the coming on them of the course of those of yore, or the coming of the torment before their eyes[1].

We sent not prophets save as heralds of glad tidings and as warners; but those who misbelieve wrangle with vain speech to make void the truth therewith; and they take my signs and the warnings given them as a jest.

[55] Who is more unjust than he who, being reminded of the signs of his Lord, turns away therefrom, and forgets what his hands have done before? verily, we will place veils upon their hearts lest they should understand, and dulness in their ears!

And if thou shouldst call them to the guidance, they will not be guided then for ever.

But thy Lord is forgiving, endowed with mercy; were He to punish them for what they have earned He would have hastened for them the torment. Nay rather, they have their appointed time, and shall never find a refuge beside Him.

These cities, we destroyed them when they were unjust; and for their destruction we set an appointed time.

And when Moses said to his servant, 'I will not cease

---

[1] This passage is aimed at the Qurâis. The 'course of those of yore' is the punishment inflicted on the 'people of Noah, Lot,' &c. for similar acts of misbelief, and 'the torment' is said to refer to their losses at the battle of Bedr.

until I reach the confluence of the two seas, or else I will go on for years[1].'

[60] But when they reached the confluence of the two[2] they forgot their fish, and it took its way in the sea with a free course.

And when they had passed by, he said to his servant, 'Bring us our dinners, for we have met with toil from this journey of ours.' Said he, 'What thinkest thou? when we resorted to the rock, then, verily, I forgot the fish, but it was only Satan who made me forget it, lest I should remember it; and it took its way in the sea wondrously!'

Said he, 'This is what we were searching for.' So they turned back upon their footsteps, following them up.

Then they found a servant of our servants, to whom we had given mercy from ourselves, and had taught him knowledge from before us. [65] Said Moses to him, 'Shall I follow thee, so that thou mayest teach me, from what thou hast been taught, the right way?' said he, 'Verily, thou canst never have patience with me. How canst thou be patient in what thou comprehendest no knowledge of?' He said, 'Thou wilt find me, if God will, patient; nor will I rebel against thy bidding.' He said, 'Then, if thou followest me, ask me not about anything until I begin for them the mention of it.'

[70] So they set out until when they rode[3] in the bark, he scuttled it.

Said he, 'Hast thou scuttled it to drown its crew? Thou hast produced a strange thing.'

---

[1] The word used signifies a space of eighty years and upwards.

[2] Literally, 'of their intermediate space.'

[3] That is, embarked. All nautical metaphors in Arabic being taken from camel riding. The Arabs do not call the camel 'the ship of the desert,' but they call a ship 'the riding camel of the sea.'

Said he, 'Did I not tell thee, verily, thou canst never have patience with me?'

Said he, 'Rebuke me not for forgetting, and impose not on me a difficult command.' So they set out until they met a boy, and he killed him. And he (Moses) said, 'Hast thou killed a pure person without (his killing) a person? thou hast produced an unheard-of thing.'

Said he, 'Did I not tell thee, verily, thou canst not have patience with me?'

[75] Said he, 'If I ask thee about anything after it, then do not accompany me. Now hast thou arrived at my excuse.' So they set out until when they came to the people of a city; and they asked the people thereof for food; but they refused to entertain them. And they found therein a wall which wanted[1] to fall to pieces, and he set it upright. Said (Moses), 'Hadst thou pleased thou mightst certainly have had a hire for this.'

Said he, 'This is the parting between me and thee. I will give thee the interpretation of that with which thou couldst not have patience. As for the bark it belonged to poor people, who toiled on the sea, and I wished to damage it, for behind it was a king who seized on every bark[2] by force. And as for the youth, his parents were believers, and we feared lest he should impose upon them rebellion and misbelief. [80] So we desired that their Lord would give them in exchange a better one than him in purity, and nearer in filial affection. And as for the wall, it belonged to two orphan youths in the city, and beneath it was a treasure belonging to them both, and their father was a righteous man,

---

[1] The expression wanted to fall is colloquial in Arabic as well as in English. Bâi*dh*âvî says, 'the expression wanting to is in this case figuratively used for being on the point of.'

[2] That is, every whole or sound ship.

and their Lord desired that they should reach puberty, and
then take out their treasure as a mercy from thy Lord; and I
did it not on my own bidding. That is the interpretation of
what thou couldst not have patience with[1].'

And they will ask thee about DHU 'l Qarâin[2], say, 'I will
recite to you a mention of him; verily, we stablished for him
in the earth, and we gave him a way to everything; and he
followed a way until when he reached the setting of the
sun, he found it setting in a black muddy spring[3], and he
found thereat a people.'

[85] We said, 'O DHU 'l Qarnâin! thou mayest either torment these people, or treat them well.' Said he, 'As for him
who does wrong, I will torment him, then shall he be sent
back to his Lord, and He will torment him with an unheard-of
torment; but as for him who believes and acts aright, for him
is an excellent reward, and we will tell him our easy bidding.'

Then he followed a way until when he reached the rising

[1] For this legend there appears to be no ancient authority whatever; the
Mohammedan commentators merely expand it, and say that El 'Hidhr (a
mythical personage, who is identified with the prophet Elias, St. George,
and the prime minister of Alexander the Great) had disappeared in search
of the water of immortality. Moses was inspired to search for him, and
told that he would find him by a rock where two seas met, and where he
should lose a fish which he was directed to take with him. Moses' servant
in the legend is Joshua, and the mysterious young man who guided him is
generally supposed to be El 'Hidhr himself, rendered immortal and super-
naturally wise by having found and drunk of the water of life.

[2] Literally, 'the two horned;' this personage is generally supposed to be
Alexander the Great, who is so represented on his coins. The Mohammedan histories of him, however, contain so many gross anachronisms,
making him, for instance, a contemporary with Moses, Abraham, &c., that
it is probable they may have confused him with some much more ancient
traditional conqueror.

[3] Probably, as Bâidhâvî suggests, the ocean, which, with its dark waters,
would remind an Arab of such a pool.

of the sun, he found it rise upon a people to whom we had given no shelter therefrom.

[90] So! And we comprehended the knowledge of what (forces) he had with him.

Then he followed a way until when he reached the point between the two mountains, he found below them both a people who could scarcely understand speech. They said, 'O DHU 'l Qarnâin! verily, Yâgûg and Mâgûg[1] are doing evil in the land. Shall we then pay thee tribute, on condition that thou set between us and them a rampart?' He said, 'What my Lord hath established me in is better; so help me with strength, and I will set between you and them a barrier.

[95] 'Bring me pigs of iron until they fill up the space between the two mountain sides.' Said he, 'Blow until it makes a fire.' Said he, 'Bring me, that I may pour over it, molten brass[2].'

So they[3] could not scale it, and they could not tunnel it.

Said he, 'This is a mercy from my Lord; but when the promise of my Lord comes to pass, He will make it as dust, for the promise of my Lord is true.'

And we left some of them to surge on that day[4] over oth-

---

[1] Gog and Magog. The people referred to appear to be tribes of the Turkomans, and the rampart itself has been identified with some ancient fortifications extending from the west coast of the Caspian to the Pontus Euxinus. The word translated mountains is the same as that translated rampart a little further on. I have, in rendering it mountains, followed the Mohammedan commentators, whose view is borne out by the subsequent mention of mountain sides.

[2] The process here described for repressing the incursions of Gog and Magog is the building of a wall of pig iron across the opening between the two mountains, fusing this into a compact mass of metal, and strengthening it by pouring molten brass over the whole.

[3] Gog and Magog.

[4] On the day of judgment, or, as some think, a little before it.

ers, and the trumpet will be blown, and we will gather them together.

[100] And we will set forth hell on that day before the misbelievers, whose eyes were veiled from my Reminder, and who were unable to hear. What! did those who misbelieve reckon that they could take my servants for patrons beside me? Verily, we have prepared hell for the misbelievers to alight in!

Say, 'Shall we inform you of those who lose most by their works? those who erred in their endeavours after the life of this world, and who think they are doing good deeds.'

[105] Those who misbelieve in the signs of their Lord and in meeting Him, vain are their works; and we will not give them right weight on the resurrection day. That is their reward,—hell! for that they misbelieved and took my signs and my apostles as a mockery.

Verily, those who believe and act aright, for them are gardens of Paradise[1] to alight in, to dwell therein for aye, and they shall crave no change therefrom.

Say, 'Were the sea ink for the words of my Lord, the sea would surely fail before the words of my Lord fail; aye, though we brought as much ink again!'

[110] Say, 'I am only a mortal like yourselves; I am inspired that your God is only one God. Then let him who hopes to meet his Lord act righteous acts, and join none in the service of his Lord.'

---

[1] Here the Persian word Firdâus is used, which has supplied the name to the abode of the blessed in so many languages.

The Chapter of Mary.

IN the name of the merciful and compassionate God.

K. H. Y. 'H. Z. The mention of thy Lord's mercy to His servant Zachariah, when he called on his Lord with a secret calling. Said he, 'My Lord! verily, my bones are weak, and my head flares with hoariness;—and I never was unfortunate in my prayers to Thee, my Lord! [5] But I fear my heirs after me, and my wife is barren; then grant me from Thee a successor, to be my heir and the heir of the family of Jacob, and make him, my Lord! acceptable.'

'O Zachariah! verily, we give thee glad tidings of a son, whose name shall be John. We never made a namesake of his before[1].'

Said he, 'My Lord! how can I have a son, when my wife is barren, and I have reached through old age to decrepitude?'

[10] He said, 'Thus says thy Lord, It is easy for Me, for I created thee at first when yet thou wast nothing.'

Said he, 'O my Lord! make for me a sign.' He said, 'Thy sign is that thou shalt not speak to men for three nights (though) sound.'

Then he went forth unto his people from the chamber, and he made signs to them: 'Celebrate (God's) praises morning and evening!'

'O John! take the Book with strength;' and we gave him

---

[1] Cf. Luke i. 61, where, however, it is said that none of Zachariah's kindred was ever before called by that name. Some commentators avoid the difficulty by interpreting the word samîyyun to mean 'deserving of the name.'

judgment when a boy, and grace from us, and purity; and he was pious and righteous to his parents, and was not a rebellious tyrant.

[15] So peace upon him the day he was born, and the day he died, and the day he shall be raised up alive.

And mention, in the Book, Mary; when she retired from her family into an eastern place; and she took a veil (to screen herself) from them; and we sent unto her our spirit; and he took for her the semblance of a well-made man. Said she, 'Verily, I take refuge in the Merciful One from thee, if thou art pious.' Said he, 'I am only a messenger of thy Lord to bestow on thee a pure boy.'

[20] Said she, 'How can I have a boy when no man has touched me, and when I am no harlot?' He said, 'Thus says thy Lord, It is easy for Me! and we will make him a sign unto man, and a mercy from us; for it is a decided matter.'

So she conceived him, and she retired with him into a remote place. And the labour pains came upon her at the trunk of a palm tree, and she said, 'O that I had died before this, and been forgotten out of mind!' and he called[1] to her from beneath her, 'Grieve not, for thy Lord has placed a stream beneath thy feet; [25] and shake towards thee the trunk of the palm tree, it will drop upon thee fresh dates fit to gather; so eat, and drink, and cheer thine eye; and if thou shouldst see any mortal say, "Verily, I have vowed to the Merciful One a fast, and I will not speak to-day with a human being." '

Then she brought it to her people, carrying it; said they, 'O Mary! thou hast done an extraordinary thing! O sister of Aaron! thy father was not a bad man, nor was thy mother a harlot!'

---

[1] Either the infant himself or the angel Gabriel; or the expression 'beneath her' may be rendered 'beneath it,' and may refer to the palm tree.

[30] And she pointed to him, and they said, ' How are we to speak with one who is in the cradle a child?' He said, 'Verily, I am a servant of God; He has brought me the Book, and He has made me a prophet, and He has made me blessed wherever I be; and He has required of me prayer and almsgiving so long as I live, and piety towards my mother, and has not made me a miserable tyrant; and peace upon me the day I was born, and the day I die, and the day I shall be raised up alive.'

[35] That is, Jesus the son of Mary,—by the word of truth whereon ye do dispute!

God could not take to himself any son! celebrated be His praise! when He decrees a matter He only says to it, 'BE,' and it is; and, verily, God is my Lord and your Lord, so worship Him; this is the right way.

And the parties have disagreed amongst themselves, but woe to those who disbelieve, from the witnessing of the mighty day! they can hear and they can see, on the day when they shall come to us; but the evildoers are to-day in obvious error!

[40] And warn them of the day of sighing, when the matter is decreed while they are heedless, and while they do not believe.

Verily, we will inherit the earth and all who are upon it, and unto us shall they return!

And mention, in the Book, Abraham; verily, he was a confessor,—a prophet. When he said to his father, 'O my sire! why dost thou worship what can neither hear nor see nor avail thee aught? O my sire! verily, to me has come knowledge which has not come to thee; then follow me, and I will guide thee to a level way.

[45] 'O my sire! serve not Satan; verily, Satan is ever a rebel against the Merciful. O my sire! verily, I fear that there

may touch thee torment from the Merciful, and that thou mayest be a client of Satan.'

Said he, 'What! art thou averse from my gods, O Abraham? verily, if thou dost not desist I will certainly stone thee; but get thee gone from me for a time!'

Said he, 'Peace be upon thee! I will ask forgiveness for thee from my Lord; verily, He is very gracious to me: but I will part from you and what ye call on beside God, and will pray my Lord that I be not unfortunate in my prayer to my Lord.'

[50] And when he had parted from them and what they served beside God, we granted him Isaac and Jacob, and each of them we made a prophet; and we granted them of our mercy, and we made the tongue of truth lofty for them[1].

And mention, in the Book, Moses; verily, he was sincere, and was an apostle,—a prophet. We called him from the right side of the mountain; and we made him draw nigh unto us to commune with him, and we granted him, of our mercy, his brother Aaron as a prophet.

[55] And mention, in the Book, Ishmael; verily, he was true to his promise, and was an apostle,—a prophet; and he used to bid his people prayers and almsgiving, and was acceptable in the sight of his Lord.

And mention, in the Book, Idrîs[2]; verily, he was a confessor,—a prophet; and we raised him to a lofty place.

These are those to whom God has been gracious, of the prophets of the seed of Adam, and of those whom we bore with Noah, and of the seed of Abraham and Israel, and of those we guided and elected; when the signs of the Merciful are read to them, they fall down adoring and weeping.

[60] And successors succeeded them, who lost sight of prayer and followed lusts, but they shall at length find

---

[1] That is, 'gave them great renown.'
[2] Generally identified with Enoch.

themselves going wrong, except such as repent and believe and act aright; for these shall enter Paradise, and shall not be wronged at all,—gardens of Eden, which the Merciful has promised to His servants in the unseen; verily, His promise ever comes to pass!

They shall hear no empty talk therein, but only 'peace;' and they shall have their provision therein, morning and evening; that is Paradise which we will give for an inheritance to those of our servants who are pious!

[65] We do not descend[1] save at the bidding of thy Lord; His is what is before us, and what is behind us, and what is between those; for thy Lord is never forgetful,—the Lord of the heavens and the earth, and of what is between the two; then serve Him and persevere in His service. Dost thou know a namesake of His?

Man will say, 'What! when I have died shall I then come forth alive? Does not man then remember that we created him before when he was naught?'

And by thy Lord! we will surely gather them together, and the devils too; then we will surely bring them forward around hell, on their knees!

[70] Then we will drag off from every sect whichever of them has been most bold against the Merciful.

Then we know best which of them deserves most to be broiled therein.

There is not one of you who will not go down to it,—that is settled and decided by thy Lord[2].

---

[1] Amongst various conjectures the one most usually accepted by the Mohammedan commentators is, that these are the words of the angel Gabriel, in answer to Mohammed's complaint of long intervals elapsing between the periods of revelation.

[2] This is interpreted by some to mean that all souls, good and bad, must pass through hell, but that the good will not be harmed. Others think it merely refers to the passage of the bridge of el Aaráf.

Then we will save those who fear us; but we will leave the evildoers therein on their knees.

And when our signs are recited to them manifest, those who misbelieve say to those who believe, 'Which of the two parties is best placed and in the best company?'

[75] And how many generations before them have we destroyed who were better off in property and appearance?

Say, 'Whosoever is in error, let the Merciful extend to him length of days!—until they see what they are threatened with, whether it be the torment or whether it be the Hour, then they shall know who is worse placed and weakest in forces!'

And those who are guided God will increase in guidance.

And enduring good works are best with thy Lord for a reward, and best for restoration.

[80] Hast thou seen him who disbelieves in our signs, and says, 'I shall surely be given wealth and children[1]?'

Has he become acquainted with the unseen, or has he taken a compact with the Merciful? Not so! We will write down what he says, and we will extend to him a length of torment, and we will make him inherit what he says, and he shall come to us alone. They take other gods besides God to be their glory. [85] Not so! They[2] shall deny their worship and shall be opponents of theirs!

Dost thou not see that we have sent the devils against the misbelievers, to drive them on to sin? but, be not thou hasty with them. Verily, we will number them a number (of

---

[1] 'Hâsîy ibn Wâil, being indebted to 'Habbâb, refused to pay him unless he renounced Mohammed. This 'Habbâb said he would never do alive or dead, or when raised again at the last day. El 'Hâsîy told him to call for his money on the last day, as he should have wealth and children then.

[2] That is, the false gods.

days),—the day when we will gather the pious to the Merciful as ambassadors, and we will drive the sinners to hell like (herds) to water! [90] They shall not possess intercession, save he who has taken a compact with the Merciful.

They say, 'The Merciful has taken to Himself a son:'—ye have brought a monstrous thing! The heavens well-nigh burst asunder thereat, and the earth is riven, and the mountains fall down broken, that they attribute to the Merciful a son! but it becomes not the Merciful to take to Himself a son! there is none in the heavens or the earth but comes to the Merciful as a servant; He counts them and numbers them by number, [95] and they are all coming to Him on the resurrection day singly.

Verily, those who believe and act aright, to them the Merciful will give love.

We have only made it easy for thy tongue that thou mayest thereby give glad tidings to the pious, and warn thereby a contentious people.

How many a generation before them have we destroyed? Canst thou find any one of them, or hear a whisper of them?

THE CHAPTER OF *T.* H.

IN the name of the merciful and compassionate God.

T. H. We have not sent down this Qur'ân to thee that thou shouldst be wretched; only as a reminder to him who fears—descending from Him who created the earth and the high heavens, the Merciful settled on the throne! [5] His are what is in the heavens, and what is in the earth, and what is between the two, and what is beneath the ground! And if thou art public in thy speech—yet, verily, he knows the secret, and more hidden still.

God, there is no god but He! His are the excellent names.

Has the story of Moses come to thee? When he saw the fire and said to his family, 'Tarry ye; verily, I perceive a fire! [10] Haply I may bring you therefrom a brand, or may find guidance by the fire[1].' And when he came to it he was called to, 'O Moses! verily, I am thy Lord, so take off thy sandals; verily, thou art in the holy valley *T*uvâ, and I have chosen thee. So listen to what is inspired thee; verily, I am God, there is no god but Me! then serve Me, and be steadfast in prayer to remember Me.

[15] 'Verily, the hour is coming, I almost make it appear[2], that every soul may be recompensed for its efforts.

---

[1] The Arabs used to light fires to guide travellers to shelter and entertainment. These fires, 'the fire of hospitality,' 'the fire of war,' &c, are constantly referred to in the ancient Arabic poetry. No less than thirteen fires are enumerated by them.

[2] This may be also rendered, 'I almost conceal it (from myself);' i'*h*fâ'un having, like many words in Arabic, two meanings directly opposite to each other. This probably arose from words being adopted into the Qurâis idiom from other dialects.

'Let not then him who believes not therein and follows his lusts ever turn thee away from therefrom, and thou be ruined.

'What is that in thy right hand, O Moses?'

Said he, 'It is my staff on which I lean, and wherewith I beat down leaves for my flocks, and for which I have other uses.'

[20] Said He, 'Throw it down, O Moses!' and he threw it down, and behold! it was a snake that moved about.

Said He, 'Take hold of it and fear not; we will restore it to its first state.

'But press thy hand to thy side, it shall come forth white without harm,—another sign! to show thee of our great signs!

[25] 'Go unto Pharaoh, verily, he is outrageous!'

Said he, 'My Lord! expand for me my breast; and make what I am bidden easy to me; and loose the knot from my tongue[1], that they may understand my speech; [30] and make for me a minister[2] from my people,—Aaron my brother; gird up my loins through him[3], and join him with me in the affair; that we may celebrate Thy praises much and remember Thee much.

[35] 'Verily, Thou dost ever behold us!'

He said, 'Thou art granted thy request, O Moses! and we have already shown favours unto thee at another time. When we inspired thy mother with what we inspired her, "Hurl him into the ark, and hurl him into the sea; and the

---

[1] The Muslim legend is that Moses burnt his tongue with a live coal when a child. This incident is related at length, together with other Mohammedan legends connected with Moses and the Exodus, in my 'Desert of the Exodus,' Appendix C. p. 533. Transl.

[2] Literally, vizîr, 'vizier,' 'one who bears the burden' of office.

[3] I.e. 'strengthen me.' The idiom is still in common use amongst the desert Arabs.

sea shall cast him on the shore, and an enemy of mine and of his shall take him;"—for on thee have I cast my love, [40] that thou mayest be formed under my eye. When thy sister walked on and said, "Shall I guide you to one who will take charge of him?" And we restored thee to thy mother, that her eye might be cheered and that she should not grieve. And thou didst slay a person and we saved thee from the trouble, and we tried thee with various trials. And thou didst tarry for years amongst the people of Midian; then thou didst come (hither) at (our) decree, O Moses! And I have chosen thee for myself. Go, thou and thy brother, with my signs, and be not remiss in remembering me. [45] Go ye both to Pharaoh; verily, he is outrageous! and speak to him a gentle speech, haply he may be mindful or may fear.'

They two said, 'Our Lord! verily, we fear that he may trespass against us, or that he may be outrageous.'

He said, 'Fear not; verily, I am with you twain. I hear and see!

'So come ye to him and say, "Verily, we are the apostles of thy Lord; send then the children of Israel with us; and do not torment them. We have brought thee a sign from thy Lord, and peace be upon him who follows the guidance!

[50]' "Verily, we are inspired that the torment will surely come upon him who calls us liars and turns his back." '

Said he, ' And who is your Lord, O Moses?'

He said, 'Our Lord is He who gave everything its creation, then guided it.'

Said he, 'And what of the former generations?'

He said, 'The knowledge of them is with my Lord in a book; my Lord misleads not, nor forgets! [55] Who made for you the earth a bed; and has traced for you paths therein; and has sent down from the sky water,—and we have brought forth thereby divers sorts of different vegetables. Eat and pasture your cattle therefrom; verily, in that are

signs to those endued with intelligence. From it have we
created you and into it will we send you back, and from it
will we bring you forth another time.'

We did show him our signs, all of them, but he called
them lies and did refuse.

Said he, 'Hast thou come to us, to turn us out of our land
with thy magic, O Moses? [60] Then we will bring you
magic like it; and we will make between us and thee an appointment; we will not break it, nor do thou either;—a fair
place.'

Said he, 'Let your appointment be for the day of adornment[1], and let the people assemble in the forenoon[2].'

But Pharaoh turned his back, and collected his tricks, and
then he came.

Said Moses to them, 'Woe to you! do not gorge against
God a lie; lest He destroy you by torment; for disappoint-
ment has ever been he who has forged.'

[65] And they argued their matter among themselves;
and secretly talked it over.

Said they, 'These twain are certainly two magicians, who
wish to turn you out of your land by their magic, and to remove your most exemplary doctrine[3]. Collect therefore
your tricks, and then form a row; for he is prosperous to-
day who has the upper hand.'

Said they, 'O Moses! either thou must throw, or we must
be the first to throw.'

He said, 'Nay, throw ye! and lo! their ropes and their
staves appeared to move along. [70] And Moses felt a secret
fear within his soul.

Said we, 'Fear not! thou shalt have the upper hand.

[1] I.e. the festival.

[2] In order that they might all see.

[3] Or, 'your most eminent men,' as some commentators interpret it, i.e.
the children of Israel.

Throw down what is in thy right hand; and it shall devour what they have made. Verily, what they have made is but a magician's trick; and no magician shall prosper wherever he comes.'

And the magicians were cast down in adoration; said they, 'We believe in the Lord of Aaron and of Moses!'

Said he[1], 'Do ye believe in Him before I give you leave? Verily, he is your master who taught you magic! Therefore will I surely cut off your hands and feet on alternate sides, and I will surely crucify you on the trunks of palm trees; and ye shall surely know which of us is keenest at torment and more lasting.'

[75] Said they, 'We will never prefer thee to what has come to us of manifest signs, and to Him who originated us. Decide then what thou canst decide; thou canst only decide in the life of this world! Verily, we believe in our Lord, that He may pardon us our sins, and the magic thou hast forced us to use; and God is better and more lasting!'

Verily, he who comes to his Lord a sinner,—verily, for him is hell; he shall not die therein, and shall not live.

But he who comes to Him a believer who has done aright—these, for them are the highest ranks,—gardens of Eden beneath which rivers flow, to dwell therein for aye; for that is the reward of him who keeps pure.

And we inspired Moses, 'Journey by night with my servants, and strike out for them a dry road in the sea. [80] Fear not pursuit, nor be afraid!' Then Pharaoh followed them with his armies, and there overwhelmed them of the sea that which overwhelmed them. And Pharaoh and his people went astray and were not guided.

O children of Israel! We have saved you from your enemy; and we made an appointment with you on the right

---

[1] Pharaoh.

side of the mount; and we sent down upon you the manna
and the quails. 'Eat of the good things we have provided
you with, and do not exceed therein, lest my wrath light
upon you; for whomsoever my wrath lights upon he falls!

'Yet am I forgiving unto him who repents and believes
and does right, and then is guided.

[85 'But what has hastened thee on away from thy people, O Moses?'

He said, 'They were here upon my track and I hastened
on to Thee, my Lord! that thou mightest be pleased.'

Said He, 'Verily, we have tried thy people, since thou
didst leave, and es Sâmarîy[1] has led them astray.'

And Moses returned to his people, wrathful, grieving!

Said he, 'O my people! did not your Lord promise you a
good promise? Has the time seemed too long for you, or do
you desire that wrath should light on you from your Lord,
that ye have broken your promise to me?'

[90] They said, 'We have not broken our promise to thee
of our own accord. But we were made to carry loads of the
ornaments of the people, and we hurled them down, and so
did es Sâmarîy cast; and he brought forth for the people a
corporeal calf which lowed.' And they said, 'This is your
god and the god of Moses, but he has forgotten!' What! do
they not see that is does not return them any speech, and
cannot control for them harm or profit? Aaron too told them
before, 'O my people! ye are only being tried thereby; and,
verily, your Lord is the Merciful, so follow me and obey my
bidding.'

They said, 'We will not cease to pay devotion to it until
Moses come back to us.'

Said he, 'O Aaron! what prevented thee, when thou didst

[1] I.e. the Samaritan; some take it to mean a proper name, in order to
avoid the anachronism.

see them go astray, from following me? Hast thou then rebelled against my bidding?'

[95] Said he, 'O son of my mother! seize me not by my beard, or my head! Verily, I feared lest thou shouldst say, "Thou hast made a division amongst the children of Israel, and hast not observed my word." '

Said he, 'What was thy design, O Sâmarîy?' Said he, 'I beheld what they beheld not, and I grasped a handful from the footprint of the messenger[1] and cast it; for thus my soul induced me.'

Said he, 'Then get thee gone; verily, it shall be thine in life to say, "Touch me not[2]!" and, verily, for thee there is a threat which thou shalt surely never alter. But look at thy god to which thou wert just now devout; we will surely burn it, and then we will scatter it in scattered pieces in the sea.

'Your God is only God who,—there is no god but He,—He embraceth everything in His knowledge.'

Thus do we narrate to thee the history of what has gone before, and we have brought thee a reminder from us.

[100] Whoso turns therefrom, verily, he shall bear on the resurrection day a burden:—for them to bear for aye, and evil for them on the resurrection day will it be to bear.

On the day when the trumpet shall be blown, and we will gather the sinners in that day blue-eyed[3].

---

[1] A handful of dust from the footprint of the angel Gabriel's horse, which, being cast into the calf, caused it to become animated and to low.

[2] The idea conveyed seems to be that he should be regarded as a leper, and obliged to warn people from coming near him. The reference is no doubt to the light in which the Samaritans (see Part II, p. 40, note 1) were regarded by the Jews.

[3] Because 'blue eyes' were especially detested by the Arabs as being characteristic of their greatest enemies, the Greeks. So they speak of an enemy as 'black-livered,' 'red-whiskered,' and 'blue-eyed.' The word in the text may also mean 'blear-eyed,' or 'blind.'

They shall whisper to each other, 'Ye have only tarried ten days.' We know best what they say, when the most exemplary of them in his way shall say, 'Ye have only tarried a day.'

[105] They will ask thee about the mountains; say, 'My Lord will scatter them in scattered pieces, and He will leave them a level of plain, thou wilt see therein no crookedness or inequality.'

On that day they shall follow the caller in whom is no crookedness[1]; and the voices shall be hushed before the Merciful, and thou shalt hear naught but a shuffling.

On that day shall no intercession be of any avail, save from such as the Merciful permits, and who is acceptable to Him in speech.

He knows what is before them and what is behind them, but they do not comprehend knowledge of Him.

[110] Faces shall be humbled before the Living, the Self-subsistent; and he who bears injustice is ever lost.

But he who does righteous acts and is a believer, he shall fear neither wrong nor diminution.

Thus have we have sent it down on Arabic Qur'ân; and we have turned about in it the threat,—haply they may fear, or it may cause them to remember.

Exalted then be God, the king, the truth! Hasten not the Qur'ân before its inspiration is decided for thee; but say, 'O Lord! increase me in knowledge.'

We did make a covenant with Adam of yore, but he forgot it, and we found no firm purpose in him.

[115] And when we said to the angels, 'Adore Adam,' they adored, save Iblîs, who refused. And we said, 'O

---

[1] That is, the angel who is to summon them to judgment, and from whom none can escape, or who marches straight on.

Adam! verily, this is a foe to thee and to thy wife; never then let him drive you twain forth from the garden or thou wilt be wretched. Verily, thou hast not to be hungry there, nor naked! and, verily, thou shalt not thirst therein, nor feel the noonday heat!'

But the devil whispered to him. Said he, 'O Adam! shall I guide thee to the tree of immortality, and a kingdom that shall not wane?'

And they eat therefrom, and their shame became apparent to them; and they began to stitch upon themselves some leaves of the garden; and Adam rebelled against his Lord, and went astray.

[120] Then his Lord chose him, and relented towards him, and guided him. Said he, 'Go down, ye twain, therefrom altogether, some of you foes to the other. And if there should come to you from me a guidance; then whoso follows my guidance shall neither err nor be wretched. But he who turns away from my reminder, verily, for him shall be a straitened livelihood; and we will gather him on the resurrection day blind!'

[125] He shall say, 'My Lord! wherefore hast Thou gathered me blind when I used to see?' He shall say, 'Our signs came to thee, and thou didst forget them; thus to-day art thou forgotten!'

Thus do we recompense him who is extravagant and believes not in the signs of his Lord; and the torment of the hereafter is keener and more lasting!

Does it not occur to them[1] how many generations we have destroyed before them?—they walk in their very dwelling-places; verily, in that are signs to those endued with intelligence.

---

[1] The Meccans.

And had it not been for thy Lord's word already passed (the punishment) would have been inevitable and (at) an appointed time.

[130] Bear patiently then what they say, and celebrate the praises of thy Lord before the rising of the sun, and before its setting, and at times in the night celebrate them; and at the ends of the day; haply thou mayest please (Him).

And do not strain after what we have provided a few[1] of them with—the flourish of the life of this world, to try them by; but the provision of thy Lord is better and more lasting.

Bid thy people prayer, and persevere in it; we do not ask thee to provide. We will provide, and the issue shall be to piety.

They say, 'Unless he bring us a sign from his Lord— What! has there not come to them the manifest sign of what was in the pages of yore?'

But had we destroyed them with torment before it, they would have said, 'Unless Thou hadst sent to us an apostle, that we might follow Thy signs before we were abased and put to shame.'

[135] Say, 'Each one has to wait, so wait ye! but in the end ye shall know who are the fellows of the level way, and who are guided!'

[1] Literally, 'pairs.'

The Chapter of the Prophets.

In the name of the merciful and compassionate God.

Their reckoning draws nigh to men, yet in heedlessness they turn aside.

No reminder comes to them from their Lord of late, but they listen while they mock, and their hearts make sport thereof! And those who do wrong discourse secretly (saying), 'Is this man aught but a mortal like yourselves? will ye accede to magic, while ye can see?'

Say, 'My Lord knows what is said in the heavens and the earth, He hears and knows!'

[5] 'Nay!' they say, '—a jumble of dreams; nay! he has forged it; nay! he is a poet; but let him bring us a sign as those of yore were sent.'

No city before them which we destroyed believed—how will they believe? Nor did we send before them any but men whom we inspired? Ask ye the people of the Scriptures if ye do not know. Nor did we make them bodies not to eat food, nor were they immortal. Yet we made our promise to them good, and we saved them and whom we pleased; but we destroyed those who committed excesses.

[10] We have sent down to you a book in which is a reminder for you; have ye then no sense?

How many a city which had done wrong have we broken up, and raised up after it another people! And when they perceived our violence they ran away from it. 'Run not away, but return to what ye delighted in, and to your dwellings! haply ye will be questioned.' Said they, 'O woe is us! verily, we were wrong-doers.'

[15] And that ceased not to be their cry until we made them mown down,—smouldering out!

We did not create the heaven and the earth and what is between the two in play. Had we wished to take to a sport, we would have taken to one from before ourselves; had we been bent on doing so. Nay, we hurl the truth against false-hood and it crashes into it, and lo! it vanishes, but woe to you for what ye attribute (to God)!

His are whosoever are in the heavens and the earth, and those who are with Him are not too big with pride for His service, nor do they weary. [20] They celebrate His praises by night and day without intermission. Or have they taken gods from the earth who can raise up (the dead)?

Were there in both (heaven and earth) gods beside God, both would surely have been corrupted. Celebrated then be the praise of God, the Lord of the throne, above what they ascribe!

He shall not be questioned concerning what He does, but they shall be questioned.

Have they taken gods beside Him? Say, 'Bring your proofs. This is the reminder of those who are with me, and of those who were before me.' Nay, most of them know not the truth, and they do turn aside.

[25] We have not sent any prophet before thee, but we in-spired him that, 'There is no god but Me, so serve ye Me.'

And they say, 'The Merciful has taken a son[1]; celebrated be His praise!'—Nay, honoured servants; they do not speak until He speaks, but at His bidding do they act. He knows what is before them, and what is behind them, and they shall not intercede except for him whom He is pleased with; and they shrink through fear.

---

[1] Or, child, since the passage refers both to the Christian doctrine and to the Arab notion that the angels are daughters of God.

[30] And whoso of them should say, 'Verily, I am god instead of Him,' such a one we recompense with hell; thus do we recompense the wrong-doers.

Do not those who misbelieve see that the heavens and the earth were both solid, and we burst them asunder; and we made from water every living thing—will they then not believe?

And we placed on the earth firm mountains lest it should move with them, and He made therein open roads for paths, haply they may be guided! and we made the heaven a guarded roof; yet from our signs they turn aside!

He it is who created the night and the day, and the sun and the moon, each floating in a sky.

[35] We never made for any mortal before thee immortality; what, if thou shouldst die, will they live on for aye?

Every soul shall taste of death! we will test them with evil and with good, as a trial; and unto us shall they return!

And when those who misbelieve see thee[1], they only take thee for a jest, 'Is this he who mentions your gods?' Yet they at the mention of the Merciful do disbelieve.

Man is created out of haste. I will show you my signs; but do not hurry Me.

And they say, 'When will this threat (come to pass), if ye tell the truth?'

[40] Did those who misbelieve but know when the fire shall not be warded off from their faces nor from their backs, and they shall not be helped! Nay, it shall come on them suddenly, and shall dumbfounder them, and they shall not be able to repel it, nor shall they be respited.

Prophets before thee have been mocked at, but that whereat they jested encompassed those who mocked.

Say, 'Who shall guard you by night and by day from the

___
[1] Mohammed.

Merciful?' Nay, but they from the mention of their Lord do turn aside.

Have they gods to defend them against us? These cannot help themselves, nor shall they be abetted against us.

[45] Nay, but we have granted enjoyment to these men and to their fathers whilst life was prolonged. Do they not see that we come to the land and shorten its borders? Shall they then prevail?

Say, 'I only warn you by inspiration;' but the deaf hear not the call when they are warned. But if a blast of the torment of thy Lord touches them, they will surely say, 'O woe is us! verily, we were wrong-doers!'

We will place just balances upon the resurrection day, and no soul shall be wronged at all, even though it be the weight of a grain of mustard seed, we will bring it; for we are good enough at reckoning up.

We did give to Moses and Aaron the Discrimination, and a light and a reminder to those who fear; [50] who are afraid of their Lord in secret; and who at the Hour do shrink.

This is a blessed reminder which we have sent down, will ye then deny it?

And we gave Abraham a right direction before; for about him we knew. When he said to his father and to his people, 'What are these images to which ye pay devotion?' Said they, 'We found our fathers serving them.' [55] Said he, 'Both you and your fathers have been in obvious error.' They said, 'Dost thou come to us with the truth, or art thou but of those who play?'

He said, 'Nay, but your Lord is Lord of the heavens and the earth, which He originated; and I am of those who testify to this; and, by God! I will plot against your idols after ye have turned and shown me your backs!'

So he brake them all in pieces, except a large one they had; that haply they might refer it to that.

[60] Said they, 'Who has done this with our gods? verily, he is of the wrong-doers!' They said, 'We heard a youth mention them who is called Abraham.'

Said they, 'Then bring him before the eyes of men; haply they will bear witness.'

Said they, 'Was it thou who did this to our gods, O Abraham?' Said he, 'Nay, it was this largest of them; but ask them, if they can speak.'

[65] Then they came to themselves and said, 'Verily, ye are the wrong-doers.' Then they turned upside down again[1]: 'Thou knewest that these cannot speak.'

Said he, 'Will ye then serve, beside God, what cannot profit you at all, nor harm you? fie upon you, and what ye serve beside God! have ye then no sense?'

Said they, 'Burn him, and help your gods, if ye are going to do so!'

We said, 'O fire! be thou cool and a safety for Abraham!'

[70] They desired to plot against him, but we made them the losers.

And we brought him and Lot safely to the land which we have blessed for the world, and we bestowed upon him Isaac and Jacob as a fresh gift, and each of them we made righteous persons; and we made them high priests to guide (men) by our bidding, and we inspired them to do good works, and to be steadfast in prayer, and to give alms; and they did serve us.

And Lot, to him we gave judgment and knowledge, and we brought him safely out of the city which had done vile acts; verily, they were a people who wrought abominations! [75] And we made him enter into our mercy; verily, he was of the righteous!

---

[1] Literally, 'they turned upside down upon their heads,' the metaphor implying that they suddenly changed their opinion and relapsed into belief in their idols.

And Noah, when he cried aforetime, and we answered him and saved him and his people from the mighty trouble, and we helped him against the people who said our signs were lies; verily, they were a bad people, so we drowned them all together.

And David and Solomon, when they gave judgment concerning the field, when some people's sheep had strayed therein at night; and we testified to their judgment[1]; and this we gave Solomon to understand. To each of them we gave judgment and knowledge; and to David we subjected the mountains to celebrate our praises, and the birds too,— it was we who did it[2].

[80] And we taught him the art of making coats of mail for you, to shield you from each other's violence; are ye then grateful?

And to Solomon (we subjected) the wind blowing stormily, to run on at his bidding to the land[3] which we have blessed,—for all things did we know,—and some devils to dive for him, and to do other works beside that; and we kept guard over them.

And Job, when he cried to his Lord, 'As for me, harm has

---

[1] This case, say the commentators, being brought before David and Solomon, David said that the owner of the field should take the sheep in compensation for the damage; but Solomon, who was only eleven years old at the time, gave judgment that the owner of the field should enjoy the produce of the sheep—that is, their milk, wool, and lambs—until the shepherd had restored the field to its former state of cultivation, and this judgment was approved by David.

[2] This legend, adopted from the Talmud, arises from a too literal interpretation of Psalm cxlviii.

[3] The legend of Solomon, his seal inscribed with the holy name by which he could control all the powers of nature, his carpet or throne that used to be transported with him on the wind wherever he pleased, his power over the ginns, and his knowledge of the language of birds and beasts are commonplaces in Arabic writings.

touched me, but Thou art the most merciful of the merciful ones.' And we answered him, and removed from him the distress that was upon him; and we gave his family, and the like of them with them, as a mercy from us, and a remembrance to those who serve us.

[85] And Ishmael, and Idrîs, and DHu 'l Kifl[1], all of these were of the patient: and we made them enter into our mercy; verily, they were among the righteous.

And DHu 'nnûn[2], when he went away in wrath and thought that we had no power over him; and he cried out in the darkness, 'There is no god but Thou, celebrated by Thy praise! Verily, I was of the evildoers!' And we answered him, and saved him from the trouble. Thus do we save believers!

And Zachariah, when he cried unto his Lord, 'O Lord! leave me not alone; for thou art the best of heirs[3].' [90] And we answered him, and bestowed upon him John; and we made his wife right for him; verily, these vied in good works, and called on us with longing and dread, and were humble before us.

And she who guarded her private parts, and we breathed into her of our Spirit, and we made her and her son a sign unto the worlds. Verily, this your nation[4] is one nation; and I am your Lord, so serve me.

But they cut up their affair amongst themselves; they all

---

[1] That is, Elias, or, as some say, Joshua, and some say Zachariah, so called because he had a portion from God Most High, and guaranteed his people, or because he had double the work of the prophets of his time and their reward; the word Kifl being used in the various senses of 'portion,' 'sponsorship,' and 'double.'—Bâidhâvî.

[2] Literally, 'he of the fish,' that is, Jonah.

[3] See Part II, p. 27.

[4] The word 'ummatun' is here used in the sense rather of 'religion, regarding the various nations and generations as each professing and repre-

shall return to us; and he who acts aright, and he who is a believer, there is no denial of his efforts, for, verily, we will write them down for him.

[95] There is a ban upon a city which we have destroyed that they shall not return, until Yâgûg and Mâgûg are let out[1], and they from every hummock[2] shall glide forth.

And the true promise draws nigh, and lo! they are staring—the eyes of those who misbelieve! O, woe is us! we were heedless of this, nay, we were wrong-doers!

Verily, ye, and what ye serve beside God, shall be the pebbles of hell, to it shall ye go down!

Had these been God's they would not have gone down thereto: but all shall dwell therein for aye; [100] for them therein is groaning, but they therein shall not be heard.

Verily, those for whom the good (reward) from us was fore-ordained, they from it shall be kept far away; they shall not hear the slightest sound thereof, and they in what their souls desire shall dwell for aye. The greatest terror shall not grieve them; and the angels shall meet them, (saying), 'This is your day which ye were promised!'

The day when we will roll up the heavens as es-Sigill rolls up the books[3]; as we produced it at its first creation will we bring it back again—a promise binding upon us; verily, we are going to do it. And already have we written in

---

senting a particular faith, and means that the religion preached to the Meccans was the same as that preached to their followers by the various prophets who are mentioned in this chapter.

[1] See Part II, p. 25.

[2] 'Hadab, some read gadath, 'grave.'

[3] Es-Sigill is the name of the angel who has charge of the book on which each human being's fate is written, which book he rolls up at a person's death. The word, however, may mean a scroll or register, and the passage may be rendered, 'like the rolling up of a scroll for writings.'

the Psalms [105] after the reminder that 'the earth shall my righteous servants inherit[1].'

Verily, in this is preaching for a people who serve me!

We have only sent thee as a mercy to the worlds.

Say, 'I am only inspired that your God is one God; are ye then resigned?' But if they turn their backs say, 'I have proclaimed (war) against all alike, but I know not if what ye are threatened with be near or far!'

[110] Verily, He knows what is spoken openly, and He knows what ye hide.

I know not, haply it is a trial for you and a provision for a season.

Say, 'My Lord! judge thou with truth! and our Lord is the Merciful whom we ask for aid against what they ascribe!'

---

[1] Psalm xxxvii. 29.

THE CHAPTER OF THE PILGRIMAGE.

In the name of the merciful and compassionate God.

O ye folk! fear your Lord. Verily, the earthquake of the Hour is a mighty thing.

On the day ye shall see it, every suckling woman shall be scared away from that to which she gave suck; and every pregnant woman shall lay down her load; and thou shalt see men drunken, though they be not drunken: but the torment of God is severe.

And amongst men is one who wrangles about God without knowledge, and follows every rebellious devil; against whom it is written down that whoso takes him for a patron, verily, he will head him astray, and will guide him towards the torment of the blaze!

[5] O ye folk! if ye are in doubt about the raising (of the dead),—verily, we created you from earth, then from a clot, then from congealed blood, then from a morsel, shaped or shapeless, that we may explain to you. And we make what we please rest in the womb until an appointed time; then we bring you forth babes; then let you reach your full age; and of you are some who die; and of you are some who are kept back till the most decrepit age, till he knows no longer aught of knowledge. And ye see the earth parched, and when we send down water on it, it stirs and swells, and brings forth herbs of every beauteous kind.

That is because God, He is the truth, and because He quickens the dead, and because He is mighty over all; and because the Hour is coming, there is no doubt therein, and because God raises up those who are in the tombs.

And amongst men is one who wrangles about God without knowledge or guidance or an illuminating book; twisting his neck from the way of God; for him is disgrace in this world, and we will make him taste, upon the resurrection day, the torment of burning.

[10] That is for what thy hands have done before, and for that God is not unjust unto His servants.

And amongst men is one who serves God (wavering) on a brink; and if there befall him good, he is comforted; but if there befall him a trial, he turns round again, and loses this world and the next—that is an obvious loss. He calls, besides God, on what can neither harm him nor profit him;—that is a wide error.

He calls on him whose harm is nigher than his profit,—a bad lord and a bad comrade.

Verily, God makes those who believe and do aright enter into gardens beneath which rivers flow; verily, God does what He will.

[15] He who thinks that God will never help him in this world or the next—let him stretch a cord to the roof[1] and put an end to himself; and let him cut it and see if his stratagem will remove what he is enraged at.

Thus have we sent down manifest signs; for, verily, God guides whom He will.

Verily, those who believe, and those who are Jews, and the Sabæns, and the Christians, and the Magians, and those who join other gods with God, verily, God will decide between them on the resurrection day; verily, God is witness over all.

Do they not see that God, whosoever is in the heavens adores Him, and whosoever is in the earth, and the sun, and the moon, and the stars, and the mountains, and the

---

[1] The word may also be rendered 'sky.'

beasts, and many among men, though many a one deserves the torments?

Whomsoever God abases there is none to honour him; verily, God does what He pleases.

[20] These are two disputants[1] who dispute about their Lord, but those who misbelieve, for them are cut out garments of fire, there shall be poured over their heads boiling water, wherewith what is in their bellies shall be dissolved and their skins too, and for them are maces of iron. Whenever they desire to come forth therefrom through pain, they are sent back into it; 'And taste ye the torment of the burning!'

Verily, God will make those who believe and do right enter into gardens beneath which rivers flow; they shall be bedecked therein with bracelets of gold and with pearls, and their garments therein shall be of silk, and they shall be guided to the goodly speech, and they shall be guided to the laudable way.

[25] Verily, those who misbelieve and who turn men away from God's path and the Sacred Mosque, which we have made for all men alike, the dweller therein, and the stranger, and he who desires therein profanation with injustice, we will make him taste grievous woe.

And when we established for Abraham the place of the House, (saying), 'Associate naught with me, but cleanse my House for those who make the circuits, for those who stand to pray, for those who bow, and for those too who adore.

'And proclaim amongst men the Pilgrimage; let them come to you on foot and on every slim camel, from every deep pass, that they may witness advantages for them, and may mention the name of God for the stated days[2] over

---

[1] Namely, the believers and the misbelievers.

[2] The first ten days of Dʜu 'l Higgeh, or the tenth day of that month,

what God has provided them with of brute beasts, then eat thereof and feed the badly off, the poor.

[30] 'Then let them finish the neglect of their persons[1], and let them pay their vows and make the circuit round the old House.

'That do. And whoso magnifies the sacred things of God it is better for him with his Lord.

'Cattle are lawful for you, except what is recited to you; and avoid the abomination of idols, and avoid speaking falsely, being 'Hanîfs to God, not associating aught with Him; for he who associates aught with God, it is as though he had fallen from heaven, and the birds snatch him up, or the wind blows him away into a far distant place.

'That—and he who makes grand the symbols[2] of God, they come from piety of heart.

'Therein have ye advantages for an appointed time, then the place for sacrificing them is at the old House.'

[35] To every nations have we appointed rites, to mention the name of God over what He has provided them with of brute beasts; and your God is one God, to Him then be resigned, and give glad tidings to the lowly, whose hearts when God is mentioned are afraid, and to those who are patient of what befalls them, and to those who are steadfast in prayer and of what we have given them expend in alms.

The bulky (camels) we have made for you one of the symbols of God, therein have ye good; so mention the name

---

when the sacrifices were offered in the vale of Minâ, and the three following days.

[1] Such as not shaving their heads and other parts of their bodies, or cutting their beards and nails, which are forbidden the pilgrim from the moment he has put on the I'hrâm, or pilgrim garb, until the offering of the sacrifice at Minâ.

[2] This means by presenting fine and comely offerings.

of God over them as they stand in a row[1], and when they fall down (dead) eat of them, and feed the easily contented and him who begs.

Thus have we subjected them to you; haply, ye may give thanks!

Their meat will never reach to God, or yet their blood, but the piety from you will reach to Him.

Thus hath He subjected them to you that ye may magnify God for guiding you: and give thou glad tidings to those who do good.

Verily, God will defend those who believe; verily, God loves not any misbelieving traitor.

[40] Permission is given to those who fight because they have been wronged,—and, verily, God to help them has the might,—who have been driven forth from their homes undeservedly, only for that they said, 'Our Lord is God;' and were it not for God's repelling some men with others, cloisters and churches and synagogues and mosques, wherein God's name is mentioned much, would be destroyed. But God will surely help him who helps Him; verily, God is powerful, mighty.

Who, if we stablish them in the earth, are steadfast in prayer, and give alms, and bid what is right, and forbid what is wrong; and God's is the future of affairs.

But if they call thee liar, the people of Noah called him liar before them, and did 'Âd and Thamûd, and the people of Abraham, and the people of Lot, and the fellows of Midian; and Moses was called a liar too: but I let the misbelievers range at large, and then I seized on them, and how great was the change!

And how many a city have we destroyed while it yet did

---

[1] Waiting to be sacrificed.

wrong, and it was turned over on its roofs, and (how many) a deserted well and lofty palace!

[45] Have they not travelled on through the land? and have they not hearts to understand with, or ears to hear with? for it is not their eyes which are blind, but blind are the hearts which are within their breasts.

They will bid thee hasten on the torment, but God will never fail in his promise; for, verily, a day with thy Lord is a thousand years of what ye number.

And to how many a city have I given full range while it yet did wrong! then I seized on it, and unto me was the return.

Say, 'O ye folk! I am naught but a plain warner to you, but those who believe and do right, for them is forgiveness and a generous provision; [50] but those who strive to discredit our signs, they are the fellows of hell!'

We have not sent before thee any apostle or prophet, but that when he wished, Satan threw not something into his wish[1]; but God annuls what Satan throws; then does God confirm his signs, and God is knowing, wise—to make what Satan throws a trial unto those in whose hearts is sickness, and those whose hearts are hard; and verily, the

---

[1] Some say that the word tamannâ means 'reading,' and the passage should then be translated, 'but that when he read Satan threw something into his reading;' the occasion on which the verse was produced being that when Mohammed was reciting the words of the Qur'ân, Chapter LIII, verses 19, 20, 'Have ye considered Allât and Al 'Huzzâ and Manât the other third?' Satan put it into his mouth to add, 'they are the two high-soaring cranes, and, verily, their intercession may be hoped for;' at this praise of their favourite idols the Qurâis were much pleased, and at the end of the recitation joined the prophet and his followers in adoration. Mohammed, being informed by the angel Gabriel of the reason for their doing so, was much concerned until this verse was revealed for his consolation. The objectionable passage was of course annulled, and the verse made to read as it now stands.

wrong-doers are in a wide schism—and that those who have been given 'the knowledge' may know that it is the truth from thy Lord, and may believe therein, and that their hearts may be lowly; for, verily, God surely will guide those who believe into a right way.

But those who misbelieve will not cease to be in doubt thereof until the Hour comes on them suddenly, or there comes on them the torment of the barren day[1].

[55] The kingdom on that day shall be God's, He shall judge between them; and those who believe and do aright shall be in gardens of pleasure, but those who misbelieve and say our signs are lies, these—for them is shameful woe.

And those who flee in God's way, and then are slain or die, God will provide them with a goodly provision; for, verily, God is the best of providers.

He shall surely make them enter by an entrance that they like; for, verily, God is knowing, clement.

That (is so). Whoever punishes with the like of what he has been injured with, and shall then be outraged again, God shall surely help him; verily, God pardons, forgives.

[60] That for that God joins on the night to the day, and joins on the day to the night, and that God is hearing, seeing; that is for that God is the truth, and for that what ye call on beside Him is falsehood, and that God is the high, the great.

Hast thou not seen that God sends down from the sky water, and on the morrow the earth is green? verily, God is kind and well aware.

His is what is in the heavens and what is in the earth; and, verily, God is rich and to be praised.

---

[1] Either 'the day of resurrection,' as giving birth to no day after it, or, 'a day of battle and defeat,' that makes mothers childless, such as the infidels experienced at Bedr.

Hast thou not seen that God has subjected for you what is in the earth, and the ship that runs on in the sea at His bidding, and He holds back the sky from falling on the earth save at His bidding[1]? verily, God to men is gracious, merciful.

[65] He it is who quickens you, then makes you die, then will He quicken you again—verily, man is indeed ungrateful.

For every nation have we made rites which they observe; let them not then dispute about the matter, but call upon thy Lord; verily, thou art surely in a right guidance!

But if they wrangle with thee, say, ' God best knows what ye do.'

God shall judge between them on the resurrection day concerning that whereon they disagreed.

Didst thou not know that God knows what is in the heavens and the earth? verily, that is in a book; verily, that for God is easy.

[70] And they serve beside God what He has sent down no power for, and what they have no knowledge of; but the wrong-doers shall have none to help them.

When our signs are read to them manifest, thou mayest recognise in the faces of those who misbelieve disdain; they well-nigh rush at those who recite to them our signs. Say, 'Shall I inform you of something worse than that for you, the Fire which God has promised to those who misbelieve? and evil journey shall it be!'

O ye folk! a parable is struck out for you, so listen to it. Verily, those on whom ye call beside God could never create a fly if they all united together to do it, and if the fly should

---

[1] As it will do at the last day. The words of the text might also be rendered 'withholds the rain,' though the commentators do not seem to notice this sense.

despoil them of aught they could not snatch it away from it—weak is both the seeker and the sought.

They do not value God at His true value; verily, God is powerful, mighty.

God chooses apostles of the angels and of men; verily, God hears and sees. [75] He knows what is before them and what is behind them; and unto God affairs return.

O ye who believe! bow down and adore, and serve your Lord, and do well, haply ye may prosper; and fight strenuously for God, as is His due. He has elected you, and has not put upon you any hindrance by your religion,—the faith of your father Abraham. He has named you Muslims before and in this (book), that the Apostle may be a witness against you, and that ye may be witnesses against men.

Be ye then steadfast in prayer, and give alms, and hold fast by God; He is your sovereign, and an excellent sovereign, and an excellent help!

THE CHAPTER OF BELIEVERS.

In the name of the merciful and compassionate God.

Prosperous are the believers who in their prayers are humble, and who from vain talk turn aside, and who in almsgiving are active. [5] And who guard their private parts—except for their wives or what their right hands possess for then, verily, they are not to be blamed;—but whoso craves aught beyond that, they are the transgressors—and who observe their trusts and convenants, and who guard well their prayers: [10] these are the heirs who shall inherit Paradise; they shall dwell therein for aye!

We have created man from an extract of clay; then we made him a clot in a sure depository; then we created the clot congealed blood, and we created the congealed blood a morsel; then we created the morsel bone, and we clothed the bone with flesh; then we produced it another creation; and blessed be God, the best of creators!

[15] Then shall ye after that surely die; then shall ye on the day of resurrection be raised.

And we have created above you seven roads[1]; nor are we heedless of the creation.

And we send down from the heaven water by measure, and we make it rest in the earth; but, verily, we are able to take it away; and we produce for you thereby gardens of palms and grapes wherein ye have many fruits, and whence ye eat.

---

[1] That is, 'seven heavens.'

[20] And a tree growing out of Mount Sinai which produces oil, and a condiment for those who eat.

And, verily, ye have a lesson in the cattle; we give you to drink of what is in their bellies; and ye have therein many advantages, and of them ye eat, and on them and on ships ye are borne!

We sent Noah unto his people, and he said, 'O my people! worship God, ye have no god but Him; do ye then not fear?'

Said the chief of those who misbelieved among his people, 'This is nothing but a mortal like yourselves who wishes to have preference over you, and had God pleased He would have sent angels; we have not heard of this amongst our fathers of yore: [25] he is nothing but a man possessed; let him bide then for a season.'

Said he, 'Help me, for they call me liar!'

And we inspired him, 'Make the ark under our eyes and inspiration; and when the oven boils over, conduct into it every kind two, with thy family, except him of them against whom the word has passed; and do not address me for those who do wrong, verily, they are to be drowned!

'But when thou art settled, thou and those with thee in the ark, say, "Praise belongs to God, who saved us from the unjust people!"

[30] 'And say, "My Lord! make me to alight in a blessed alighting-place, for Thou art the best of those who cause men to alight!" ' Verily, in that is a sign, and, verily, we were trying them.

Then we raised up after them another generation; and we sent amongst them a prophet of themselves (saying), 'Serve God, ye have no god but He; will ye then not fear?'

Said the chiefs of his people who misbelieved, and called the meeting of the last day a lie, and to whom we gave enjoyment in the life of this world, 'This is only a mortal like yourselves, who eats of what ye eat, [35] and drinks of what ye drink; and if ye obey a mortal like yourselves, verily, ye will then be surely losers! Does he promise you that when ye are dead, and have become dust and bones, that then ye will be brought forth?

'Away, away with what ye are threatened,—there is only our life in the world! We die and we live, and we shall not be raised! [40] He is only a man who forges against God a lie. And we believe not in him!'

Said he, 'My Lord! help me, for they call me liar!' He said, 'Within a little they will surely awake repenting!'

And the noise seized them deservedly; and we made them as rubbish borne by a torrent; so, away with the unjust people!

Then we raised up after them other generations.

[45] No nation can anticipate its appointed time, nor keep it back.

Then we sent our apostles one after another. Whenever its apostle came to any nation they called him a liar; and we made some to follow others; and we made them legends; away then with a people who do not believe!

Then we sent Moses and his brother Aaron with our signs, and with plain authority to Pharaoh and his chiefs, but they were too big with pride, and were a haughty people.

And they said, 'Shall we believe two mortals like ourselves, when their people are servants of ours?'

[50] So they called them liars, and were of those who perished.

And we gave Moses the Book, that haply they might be guided.

And we made the son of Mary and his mother a sign; and we lodged them both on a high place, furnished with security and a spring.

O ye apostles! eat of the good things and do right; verily, what ye do I know!

And, verily, this nation[1] of yours is one nation, and I am your Lord; so fear me.

[55] And they have become divided as to their affair amongst themselves into sects[2], each party rejoicing in what they have themselves. So leave them in their flood (of error) for a time.

Do they reckon that that of which we grant them such an extent, of wealth and children, we hasten to them as good things—nay, but they do not perceive!

Verily, those who shrink with terror at their Lord, [60] and those who in the signs of their Lord believe, and those who with their Lord join none, and those who give what they do give while their hearts are afraid that they unto their Lord will return,—these hasten to good things and are first to gain the same. But we will not oblige a soul beyond its capacity; for with us is a book that utters the truth, and they shall not be wronged.

[65] Nay, their hearts are in a flood (of errors) at this, and they have works beside this which they do[3]. Until we catch the affluent ones amongst them with the torment; then lo! they cry for aid.

Cry not for aid to-day! verily, against us ye will not be helped. My signs were recited to you, but upon your heels did ye turn back, big with pride at it[4], in vain discourse by night.

[70] Is it that they did not ponder over the words, whether that has come to them which came not to their fathers of

---

[1] Or, 'religion.'

[2] Literally, 'into Scriptures,' i.e. into sects, each appealing to a particular book.

[3] I.e. their works are far different from the good works just described.

[4] At their possession of the Kaabah. The Qurâis are meant.

yore? Or did they not know their apostle, that they thus deny him? Or do they say, 'He is possessed by a ginn?' Nay, he came to them with the truth, and most of them are averse from the truth.

But if the truth were to follow their lusts, the heavens and the earth would be corrupted with all who in them are!— Nay, we brought them their reminder, but they from their reminder turn aside.

Or dost thou ask them for a tribute? but the tribute of thy Lord is better, for He is the best of those who provide.

[75] And, verily, thou dost call them to a right way; but, verily, those who believe not in the hereafter from the way do veer.

But if we had mercy on them, and removed the distress[1] they have, they would persist in their rebellion, blindly wandering on!

And we caught them with the torment[2], but they did not abase themselves before their Lord, nor did they humble themselves; until we opened for them a door with grievous torment, then lo! they are in despair.

[80] He it is who produced for you hearing, and sight, and minds,—little is it that ye thank. And He it is who created you in the earth, and unto Him shall ye be gathered. And He it is who gives you life and death; and His is the alteration of the night and the day; have ye then no sense?

Nay, but they said like that which those of yore did say. They said, 'What! when we have become earth and bones, are we then going to be raised? [85] We have been promised this, and our fathers too, before;—this is naught but old folks' tales!'

---

[1] The famine which the Meccans suffered; and which was attributed to Mohammed's denunciations.

[2] Their defeat at Bedr.

Say, 'Whose is the earth and those who are therein, if ye but know?'

They will say, 'God's.' Say, 'Do ye not then mind?'

Say, 'Who is Lord of the seven heavens, and Lord of the mighty throne?'

They will say, 'God.' Say, 'Do ye not then fear?'

[90] Say, 'In whose hand is the dominion of everything; He succours but is not succoured,—if ye did but know?'

They will say, 'God's.' Say, 'Then how can ye be so infatuated?'

Nay, we have brought them the truth, but, verily, they are liars!

God never took a son, nor was there ever any god with Him;—then each god would have gone off with what he had created, and some would have exalted themselves over others,—celebrated be His praises above what they attribute (to Him)!

He who knows the unseen and the visible, exalted be He above what they join with Him!

[95] Say, 'My Lord! if Thou shouldst show me what they are threatened,—my Lord! then place me not amongst the unjust people.'

Repel evil by what is better[1]. We know best what they attribute (to thee). And say, 'My Lord! I seek refuge in Thee from the incitings of the devils; [100] and I seek refuge in Thee from their presence!'

Until when death comes to any one of them he says, 'My Lord! send ye me back[2], haply I may do right in that which I have left!'

---

[1] I.e. by doing good for evil, provided that the cause of Islâm suffers nothing from it.

[2] I.e. back to life. The plural is used 'by way of respect,' say the commentators.

Not so!—a mere word he speaks!—but behind them is a bar until the day they shall be raised.

And when the trumpet shall be blown, and there shall be no relation between them on that day, nor shall they beg of each other then!

[105] And he whose scales are heavy,—they are the prosperous. But he whose scales are light,—these are they who lose themselves, in hell to dwell for aye! The fire shall scorch their faces, and they shall curl their lips therein! 'Were not my signs recited to you? and ye said that they were lies!' They say, 'Our Lord! our misery overcame us, and we were people who did err! Our Lord! take us out therefrom, and if we return[1], then shall we be unjust.'

[110] He will say, 'Go ye away into it and speak not to me!'

Verily, there was a sect of my servants who said, 'Our Lord! we believe, so pardon us, and have mercy upon us, for Thou art the best of the merciful ones.'

And ye took them for a jest until ye forgat my reminder and did laugh thereat. Verily, I have recompensed them this day for their patience; verily, they are happy now.

He will say, 'How long a number of years did ye tarry on earth?' [115] They will say, 'We tarried a day or part of a day, but ask the Numberers[2].'

He will say, 'Ye have only tarried a little, were ye but to know it. Did ye then reckon that we created you for sport, and that to us ye would not return?' But exalted be God, the true; there is no god but He, the Lord of the noble throne! and whoso calls upon another god with God has no proof of it, but, verily, this account is with his Lord; verily, the misbelievers shall not prosper. And say, 'Lord, pardon and be merciful, for Thou art the best of the merciful ones!'

[1] To our evil ways.
[2] That is, the recording angels.

THE CHAPTER OF LIGHT.

In the name of the merciful and compassionate God.

A chapter which we have sent down and determined, and have sent down therein manifest signs; haply ye may be mindful.

The whore and the whoremonger. Scourge each of them with a hundred stripes, and do not let pity for them take hold of you in God's religion, if ye believe in God and the last day; and let a party of the believers witness their torment. And the whoremonger shall marry none but a whore or an idolatress; and the whore shall none marry but an adulterer or an idolater; God has prohibited this to the believers; but those who cast (imputations) on chaste women and then do not bring four witnesses, scourge them with eighty stripes, and do not receive any testimony of theirs ever, for these are the workers of abomination. [5] Except such as repent after that and act aright, for, verily, God is forgiving and compassionate.

And those who cast (imputation) on their wives and have no witnesses except themselves, then the testimony of one of them shall be to testify four times that, by God, he is of those who speak the truth; and the fifth testimony shall be that the curse of God shall be on him if he be of those who lie. And it shall avert the punishment from her if she bears testimony four times that, by God, he is of those who lie; and the fifth that the wrath of God shall be on her if he be of those who speak the truth.

[10] And were it not for God's grace upon you and His mercy, and that God is relenting, wise . . .[1]

Verily, those who bring forward the lie, a band of you,— reckon it not as an evil for you, nay, it is good for you; every man of them shall have what he has earned of sin; and he of them who managed to aggravate it, for him is mighty woe[2].

Why did not, when ye heard it, the believing men and believing women think good in themselves, and say, 'This is an obvious lie?' Why did they not bring four witnesses to it? but since they did not bring the witnesses, then they in God's eyes are the liars. And but for God's grace upon you, and His mercy in this world and the next, there would have touched you, for that which ye spread abroad, mighty woe. When ye reported it with your tongues, and spake with your mouths what ye had no knowledge of, and reckoned it a light thing, while in God's eyes it was grave.

[15] And why did ye not say when ye heard it, 'It is not for us to speak of this? Celebrated be His praises, this is a mighty calumny!'

God admonishes you that ye return not to the like of it

---

[1] He would punish you.

[2] This passage and what follows refers to the scandal about Mohammed's favourite wife Ayesha, who, having been accidentally left behind when the prophet and his followers were starting at night on an expedition, in the sixth year of the Hiǧrah, was brought on to the camp in the morning by Zafwân ibn de Mu'haṭṭal: this gave rise to rumours derogatory to Ayesha's character, which these verses are intended to refute. Ayesha never forgave those who credited the reports against her innocence, and 'Ali, who had spoken in a disparaging manner of her on the occasion, so seriously incurred her displeasure that she contrived to bring about the ruin of his family, and the murder of his two sons Hasan and Husein; the principal parties concerned in the actual spread of the calumny were punished with the fourscore stripes above ordained, with the exception of the ringleader, Abdallah ibn Ubbâi, who was too important a person to be so treated.

ever, if ye be believers; and God manifests to you the signs, for God is knowing, wise.

Verily, those who love that scandal should go abroad amongst those who believe, for them is grievous woe in this world and the next; for God knows, but ye do not know.

[20] And but for God's grace upon you, and His mercy, and that God is kind and compassionate . . . !

O ye who believe! follow not the footsteps of Satan, for he who follows the footsteps of Satan, verily, he bids you sin and do wrong; and but for God's grace upon you and His mercy, not one of you would be ever pure; but God purifies whom He will, and for God both hears and knows. And let not those amongst you who have plenty and ample means swear that they will not give aught to their kinsman and the poor[1] and those who have fled their homes in God's way, but let them pardon and pass it over. Do ye not like God to forgive you? and God is forgiving, compassionate.

Verily, those who cast imputations on chaste women who are negligent but believing shall be cursed in this world and the next; and for them is mighty woe. The day when their tongues and hands and feet shall bear witness against them of what they did, on [25] that day God will pay them their just due; and they shall know that God, He is the plain truth.

The vile women to the vile men, and the vile men to the vile women; and the good women to the good men, and the good men to the good women: these are clear of what they say to them—forgiveness and a noble provision!

O ye who believe! enter not into houses which are not your own houses, until ye have asked leave and saluted the people thereof, that is better for you; haply ye may be mind-

---

[1] Abu bekr had sworn not to do anything more for a relation of his, named Misṭaʿh, who had taken part in spreading the reports against Ayesha.

ful. And if ye find no one therein, then do not enter them until permission is given you, and if it be said to you, 'Go back!' then go back, it is purer for you; for God of what ye do doth know. It is no crime against you that ye enter uninhabited houses,—a convenience for you;—and God knows what ye show and what ye hide.

[30] Say to the believers that they cast down their looks and guard their private parts; that is purer for them; verily, God is well aware of what they do.

And say to the believing women that they cast down their looks and guard their private parts, and display not their ornaments, except those which are outside; and let them pull their kerchiefs over their bosoms and not display their ornaments save to their husbands and fathers, or the fathers of their husbands, or their sons, or the sons of their husbands, or their brothers, or their brothers' sons, or their sisters' sons, or their women, or what their right hands possess, or their male attendants who are incapable[1], or to children who do not note women's nakedness; and that they beat not with their feet that their hidden ornaments may be known[2];—but turn ye all repentant to God, O ye believers! haply ye may prosper.

And marry the single amongst you, and the righteous among your servants and your handmaidens. If they be poor, God will enrich them of His grace, for God both comprehends and knows. And let those who cannot find a match, until God enriches them of His grace, keep chaste.

And such of those whom your right hands possess as crave a writing[3], write it for them, if ye know any good in

---

[1] Or, according to some, of deficient intellect.

[2] I.e. they are not to tinkle their bangles or ankle-rings.

[3] I.e. a document allowing them to redeem themselves on payment of a certain sum.

them, and give them of the wealth of God which He has given you. And do not compel your slave girls to prostitution, if they desire to keep continent, in order to crave the goods of the life of this world; but he who does compel them, then, verily, God after they are compelled is forgiving, compassionate[1].

Now have we sent down to you manifest signs, and the like of those who have passed away before you[2], and as an admonition to those who fear.

[35] God is the light of the heavens and the earth; His light is as a niche in which is a lamp, and the lamp is in a glass, the glass is as though it were a glittering star; it is lit from a blessed tree, an olive neither of the east nor of the west, the oil of which would well-nigh give light though no fire touched it,—light upon light!—God guides to His light whom He pleases; and God strikes out parables for men, and God all things doth know.

In the houses God has permitted to be reared and His name to be mentioned therein—His praises are celebrated therein mornings and evenings.

Men whom neither merchandize nor selling divert from the remembrance of God and steadfastness in prayer and giving alms, who fear a day when hearts and eyes shall be upset;—that God may recompense them for the best that they have done, and give them increase of His grace; for God provides whom He pleases without count.

But those who misbelieve, their works are like the mirage in a plain, the thirsty counts it water till when he comes to it

---

[1] Abdallah ibn Ubbâi, mentioned in Part II, p. 74, note 2, had six slave girls whom he compelled to live by prostitution. One of them complained to Mohammed, whence this passage.

[2] I.e. like the stories of Joseph, Part I, p. 221, and the Virgin Mary, Part II, p. 29, both of whom, like Ayesha, were accused of incontinence, and miraculously proved innocent.

he finds nothing, but he finds that God is with him; and He will pay him his account, for God is quick to take account.

[40] Or like darkness on a deep sea, there covers it a wave above which is a wave, above which is a cloud,—darkness one above the other,—when one puts out his hand he can scarcely see it; for he to whom God has given no light, he had no light.

Hast thou not seen that God,—all who are in the heavens and the earth celebrate His praises, and the birds too spreading out their wings; each one knows its prayer and its praise, and God knows what they do?

Hast thou not seen that God drives the clouds, and then re-unites them, and then accumulates them, and thou mayest see the rain coming forth from their midst; and He sends down from the sky mountains[1] with hail therein, and He makes it fall on whom He pleases, and He turns it from whom He pleases; the flashing of His lightning well-nigh goes off with their sight?

God interchanges the night and the day; verily, in that is a lesson to those endowed with sight.

And God created every beast from water, and of them is one that walks upon its belly, and of them one that walks upon two feet, and of them one that walks upon four. God creates what He pleases; verily, God is mighty over all!

[45] Now have we sent down manifest signs, and God guides whom He pleases unto the right way.

They will say, 'We believe in God and in the Apostle, and we obey.' Then a sect of them turned their backs after that, and they are not believers.

And when they are called to God and His Apostle to judge between them, lo! a sect of them do turn aside. But

---

[1] I.e. masses of cloud as large as mountains.

had the right been on their side they would have come to him submissively enough.

Is there a sickness in their hearts, or do they doubt, or do they fear lest God and His Apostle should deal unfairly by them?—Nay, it is they who are unjust.

[50] The speech of the believers, when they are called to God and His Apostle to judge between them, is only to say, 'We hear and we obey;' and these it is who are the prosperous, for whoso obeys God and His Apostle and dreads God and fears Him, these it is who are the happy.

They swear by God with their most strenuous oath that hadst Thou ordered them they would surely go forth. Say, 'Do not swear—reasonable obedience[1]; verily, God knows what ye do.'

Say, 'Obey God and obey the Apostle; but if ye turn your backs he has only his burden to bear, and ye have only your burden to bear. But if ye obey him, ye are guided; but the Apostle has only his plain message to deliver.'

God promises those of you who believe and do right that He will give them the succession in the earth as He gave the succession to those before them, and He will establish for them their religion which He has chosen for them, and to give them, after their fear, safety in exchange;—they shall worship me, they shall not associate aught with me: but whoso disbelieves after that, those it is who are the sinners.

[55] And be steadfast in prayer and give alms and obey the Apostle, haply ye may obtain mercy.

Do not reckon that those who misbelieve can frustrate

---

[1] The construction of the original is vague, and the commentators themselves make but little of it. The most approved rendering, however, seems to be either that obedience is the reasonable course to pursue, and not the mere swearing to obey.

(God) in the earth, for their resort is the Fire, and an ill journey shall it be.

O ye who believe! let those whom your right hands possess, and those amongst you who have not reached puberty, ask leave of you three times: before the prayer of dawn, and when ye put off your clothes at noon, and after the evening prayer;—three times of privacy for you[1]: there is no crime on either you or them after these while ye are continually going one about the other. Thus does God explain to you His signs, for God is knowing, wise.

And when your children reach puberty let them ask leave as those before them asked leave. Thus does God explain to you His signs, for God is knowing, wise.

And those women who have stopped (child-bearing), who do not hope for a match, it is no crime on them that they put off their clothes so as not to display their ornaments; but that they abstain is better for them, for God both hears and knows.

[60] There is no hindrance to the blind, and no hindrance to the lame, and no hindrance to the sick, and none upon yourselves that you eat from your houses, or the houses of your fathers, or the houses of your mothers, or the houses of your brothers, or the houses of your sisters, or the houses of your paternal uncles, or the houses of your paternal aunts, or the houses of your maternal uncles, or the houses of your maternal aunts, or what ye possess the keys of, or of your friend, there is no crime on you that ye eat all together or separately[2].

---

[1] I.e. at the times when persons are undressed, namely, to rise in the morning, to sleep at noon, and to retire for the night, their attendants and children must not come in without first asking permission.

[2] The Arabs in Mohammed's time were superstitiously scrupulous about eating in any one's house but their own.

And when ye enter houses then greet each other with a salutation from God, blessed and good. Thus does God explain to you His signs, haply ye may understand.

Only those are believers who believe in God and His Apostle, and when they are with Him upon public business go not away until they have asked his leave; verily, those who ask thy leave they it is who believe in God and His Apostle.

But when they ask thy leave for any of their own concerns, then give leave to whomsoever thou wilt of them, and ask pardon for them of God; verily, God is forgiving and merciful.

Make not the calling of the Apostle amongst yourselves like your calling one to the other[1]; God knows those of you who withdraw themselves covertly. And let those who disobey his order beware lest there befall them some trial or there befall them grievous woe. Ay, God's is what is in the heavens and the earth, He knows what ye are at; and the day ye shall be sent back to Him then He will inform you of what ye have done, for God all things doth know.

[1] That is, do not address the prophet without some respectful title.

The Chapter of the Discrimination[1].

In the name of the merciful and compassionate God. Blessed be He who sent down the Discrimination to His servant that he might be unto the world a warner; whose is the kingdom of the heavens and the earth, and who has not taken to Himself a son, and who has no partner in His kingdom, and created everything, and then decreed it determinately! And they take beside Him gods who create not aught, but are themselves created, and cannot control for themselves harm or profit, and cannot control death, or life, or resurrection.

[5] And those who misbelieve say, 'This is nothing but a lie which he has forged, and another people hath helped him at it;' but they have wrought an injustice and a falsehood.

And they say, 'Old folks' tales, which he has got written down while they are dictated to him morning and evening.'

Say, 'He sent it down who knows the secret in the heavens and the earth; verily, He is ever forgiving, merciful!'

And they say, 'What ails this prophet that he eats food and walks in the markets?—unless there be sent down to him an angel and be a warner with him . . . Or there be thrown to him a treasury, or he have a garden to eat therefrom. . . . !' and the unjust say, 'Ye only follow an infatuated man.'

[10] See how they strike out for thee parables, and err, and cannot find a way.

[1] In Arabic Al Furqân, which is one of the names of the Qur'ân.

Blessed be He who, if He please, can make for thee better than that, gardens beneath which rivers flow, and can make for thee castles!

Nay, but they call the Hour a lie; but we have prepared for those who call the Hour a lie a blaze: when it seizes them from a far-off place they shall hear its raging and roaring; and when they are thrown into a narrow place thereof, fastened together, they shall call there for destruction.

[15] Call not to-day for one destruction, but call for many destructions!

Say, 'Is that better or the garden of eternity which was promised to those who fear—which is ever for them a recompense and a retreat?' They shall have therein what they please, to dwell therein for aye: that is of thy Lord a promise to be demanded.

And the day He shall gather them and what they served beside God, and He shall say, 'Was it ye who led my servants here astray, or did they err from the way?'

They shall say, 'Celebrated be Thy praise, it was not befitting for us to take any patrons but Thee; but Thou didst give them and their fathers enjoyment until they forgot the Reminder and were a lost people!'

[20] And now have they proved you liars for what ye say, and they[1] cannot ward off or help. And he of you who does wrong we will make him taste great torment.

We have not sent before thee any messengers but that they ate food and walked in the markets; but we have made some of you a trial to others: will ye be patient? thy Lord doth ever look.

And those who do not hope to meet us say, 'Unless the angels be sent down to us, or we see our Lord. . . . !' They

---

[1] Another reading of the text is, 'ye cannot.'

are too big with pride in their souls and they have exceeded with a great excess!

The day they shall see the angels,—no glad tidings on that day for the sinners, and they shall say, 'It is rigorously forbidden[1]!'

[25] And we will go on to the works which they have done, and make them like motes in a sunbeam scattered! The fellows of Paradise on that day shall be in a better abiding-place and a better noonday rest.

The day the heavens shall be cleft asunder with the clouds, and the angels shall be sent down descending.

The true kingdom on that day shall belong to the Merciful, and it shall be a hard day for the misbelievers.

And the day when the unjust shall bite his hands and say, 'O, would that I had taken a way with the Apostle[2]! [30] O, woe is me! would that I had not taken such a one for a friend now, for he did lead me astray from the Reminder after it had come to me, for Satan leaves man in the lurch!'

The Apostle said, 'O my Lord! verily, my people have taken this Qur'ân to be obsolete!'

Thus have we made for every prophet an enemy from among the sinners; but thy Lord is good guide and helper enough.

Those who misbelieve said, 'Unless the Qur'ân be sent down to him all at once[3]. . . . !'—thus—that we may stablish

---

[1] The ancient Arabs used this formula when they met an enemy during a sacred month, and the person addressed would then abstain from hostilities. The sinners in this passage are supposed to use it to the angels, but without effect. Some commentators take it to mean that the 'glad tidings' are 'rigorously forbidden,' and that the angels are the speakers.

[2] That is, followed him.

[3] Like the Pentateuch and Gospels, which were revealed all at once, according to the Mohammedan tradition.

thy heart therewith, did we reveal it piecemeal[1]. [35] Nor shall they come to thee with a parable without our bringing thee the truth and the best interpretation.

They who shall be gathered upon their faces to hell,—these are in the worst place, and err most from the path.

And we did give to Moses the Book, and place with him his brother Aaron as a minister; and we said, 'Go ye to the people who say our signs are lies, for we will destroy them with utter destruction.'

And the people of Noah, when they said the apostles were liars, we drowned them, and we made them a sign for men; and we prepared for the unjust a grievous woe.

[40] And 'Âd and Thamûd and the people of ar Rass[2], and many generations between them.

For each one have we struck out parables, and each one have we ruined with utter ruin.

Why, they[3] have come past the cities which were rained on with an evil rain; have they not seen them?—nay, they do not hope to be raised up again.

And when they saw thee they only took thee for a jest, 'Is this he whom God has sent as an apostle? he well-nigh leads us astray from our gods, had we not been patient about them.' But they shall know, when they see the torment, who errs most from the path. [45] Dost thou consider him who takes his lusts for his god? wilt thou then be in charge over him? or dost thou reckon that most of them will

---

[1] Or it may be rendered, 'slowly and distinctly;' the whole revelation of the Qur'ân extends over a period of twenty-three years.

[2] The commentators do not know where to place ar Rass; some say it was a city in Yamâmah, others that it was a well near Midian, and others again that it was in 'Hadhramaut.

[3] That is, the idolatrous Meccans; see Part I, p. 249, note 2.

hear or understand? they are only like the cattle, nay, they err more from the way.

Hast thou not looked to thy Lord how He prolongs the shadow? but had He willed He would have made it stationary; then we make the sun a guide thereto, then we contract it towards us with an easy contraction.

And He it is who made the night for a garment; and sleep for repose, and made the day for men to rise up again. [50] And He it is who sent the winds with glad tidings before His mercy; and we send down from the heavens pure water, to quicken therewith the dead country, and to give it for drink to what we have created,—the cattle and many folk.

We have turned it[1] in various ways amongst them that they may remember; though most men refuse aught but to misbelieve. But, had we pleased, we would have sent in every city a warner. So obey not the unbelievers and fight strenuously with them in many a strenuous fight.

[55] He it is who has let loose the two seas, this one sweet and fresh, that one bitter and pungent, and has made between them a rigorous prohibition.

And He it is who has created man from water, and has made for him blood relationship and marriage relationship; for thy Lord is mighty.

Yet they worship beside God what can neither profit them nor harm them; but he who misbelieves in his Lord backs up (the devil).

We have only sent thee to give glad tidings and to warn. Say, 'I ask you not for it a hire unless one please to take unto his Lord a way[2].' [60] And rely thou upon the Living One

---

[1] That is, either the Qur'ân, cf. Part II, p. 5, line 25; or the words may be rendered, 'We distribute it' (the rain), &c.

[2] That is, that if a man chose to expend anything for the cause of God he can do so.

who dies not; and celebrate His praise, for He knows well enough about the thoughts of His servants. He who created the heavens and the earth, and what is between them, in six days, and then made for the throne; the Merciful One, ask concerning Him of One who is aware.

And when it is said, 'Adore ye the Merciful!' they say, 'What is the Merciful? shall we adore what thou dost order us?' and it only increases their aversion.

Blessed be He who placed in the heavens zodiacal signs, and placed therein the lamp and an illuminating moon!

And He it is who made the night and the day alternating for him who desires to remember or who wishes to be thankful.

And the servants of the Merciful are those who walk upon the earth lowly, and when the ignorant address them, say, 'Peace!' [65] And those who pass the night adoring their Lord and standing[1]; and those who say, 'O our Lord! turn from us the torment of hell; verily, its torments are persistent; verily, they are evil as an abode and a station.'

And those who when they spend are neither extravagant nor miserly, but who ever take their stand between the two; and who call not upon another god with God; and kill not the soul which God has prohibited save deservedly; and do not commit fornication: for he who does that shall meet with a penalty; doubled for him shall be the torment on the resurrection day, and he shall be therein for aye despised. [70] Save he who turns again and believes and does a righteous work; for, as to those, God will change their evil deeds to good, for God is ever forgiving, merciful.

And he who turns again and does right, verily, he turns again to God repentant.

And those who do not testify falsely; and when they pass

[1] For prayer.

by frivolous discourse, pass by it honourably; and those who when they are reminded of the signs of their Lord do not fall down thereat deaf and blind; and those who say, 'Our Lord! grant us from our wives and seed that which may cheer our eyes and make us models to the pious!'

[75] These shall be rewarded with a high place[1] for that they were patient: and they shall meet therein with salutation and peace,—to dwell therein for aye; a good abode and station shall it be!

Say, 'My Lord cares not for you though you should not call (on Him); and ye have called (the Apostle) a liar, but it shall be (a punishment) which ye cannot shake off.'

---

[1] In Paradise.

THE CHAPTER OF THE POETS.
(XXVI. Mecca.)

IN the name of the merciful and compassionate God.

T. S. M. Those are the signs of the perspicuous Book; haply thou art vexing thyself to death that they will not be believers!

If we please we will send down upon them from the heaven a sign, and their necks shall be humbled thereto. But there comes not to them any recent Reminder from the Merciful One that they do not turn away from. [5] They have called (thee) liar! but there shall come to them a message of that at which they mocked.

Have they not looked to the earth, how we caused to grow therein of every noble kind? verily, in that is a sign; but most of them will never be believers! but, verily, thy Lord He is mighty and merciful.

And when thy Lord called Moses (saying), 'Come to the unjust people, [10] to the people of Pharaoh, will they not fear?' Said he, 'My lord! verily, I fear that they will call me liar; and my breast is straitened, and my tongue is not fluent; send then unto Aaron[1], for they have a crime against me, and I fear that they may kill me[2]. Said He, 'Not so; but go with our signs, verily, we are with you listening.

[15] 'And go to Pharaoh and say, "Verily, we are the apostles of the Lord of the worlds (to tell thee to) send with us the children of Israel." '

---

[1] That he may be my minister.
[2] The slaying of the Egyptian.

And he said, 'Did we not bring thee up amongst us as a child? and thou didst dwell amongst us for years of thy life; and thou didst do they deed which thou hast done, and thou art of the ungrateful!'

Said he, 'I did commit this, and I was of those who erred.

[20] 'And I fled from you when I feared you, and my Lord granted me judgment, and made me one of His messengers; and this is the favour thou hast obliged me with, that thou hast enslaved the children of Israel!'

Said Pharaoh, 'Who is the Lord of the worlds?' Said he, 'The lord of the heavens and the earth and what is between the two, if ye are but sure.'

Said he to those about him, 'Do ye not listen?' [25] Said he, 'Your lord and the Lord of your fathers of yore!'

Said he, 'Verily, your apostle who is sent to you is surely mad!'

Said he, 'The Lord of the east and of the west, and of what is between the two, if ye had but sense!'

Said he, 'If thou dost take a god besides Me I will surely make thee one of the imprisoned!'

Said he, 'What, if I come to thee with something obvious?'

[30] Said he, 'Bring it, if thou art of those who tell the truth!'

And he threw down his rod, and, behold, it was an obvious serpent! and he plucked out his hand, and, behold, it was white to the spectators!

He[1] said to the chiefs around him, 'Verily, this is a knowing sorcerer, he desires to turn you out of your land! what is it then ye bid?'

[35] They said, 'Give him and his brother some hope, and send into the cities to collect and bring to thee every knowing sorcerer.'

---

[1] Pharaoh.

And the sorcerers assembled at the appointed time on a stated day, and it was said to the people, 'Are ye assembled? haply we may follow the sorcerers if we gain the upper hand.'

[40] And when the sorcerers came they said to Pharaoh, 'Shall we, verily, have a hire if we gain the upper hand?' Said he, 'Yes; and, verily, ye shall then be of those who are nigh (my throne).' And Moses said to them, 'Throw down what ye have to throw down.' So they threw down their ropes and their rods and said, 'By Pharaoh's might, verily, we it is who shall gain the upper hand!'

And Moses threw down his rod, and, lo, it swallowed up what they falsely devised!

[45] And the sorcerers threw themselves down, adoring. Said they, 'We believe in the Lord of the worlds, the Lord of Moses and Aaron!' Said he, 'Do ye believe in Him ere I give you leave? Verily, he is your chief who has taught you sorcery, but soon ye shall know. I will surely cut off your hands and your feet from opposite sides, and I will crucify you all together!'

[50] They said, 'No harm; verily, unto our Lord do we return! verily, we hope that our Lord will forgive us our sins, for we are the first of believers!'

And we inspired Moses, 'Journey by night with my servants; verily, ye are pursued.'

And Pharaoh sent into the cities to collect; 'Verily, these are a small company. [55] And, verily, they are enraged with us; but we are a multitude, wary!

'Turn them out of gardens and springs, and treasuries, and a noble station!'—thus,—and we made the children of Israel to inherit them.

[60] And they followed them at dawn; and when the two hosts saw each other, Moses' companions said, 'Verily, we

are overtaken!' Said he, 'Not so; verily, with me is my Lord, He will guide me.'

And we inspired Moses, 'Strike with thy rod the sea;' and it was cleft asunder, and each part was like a mighty mountain. And then we brought the others. [65] And we saved Moses and those with him all together; then we drowned the others; and that is a sign: but most of them will never be believers! And, verily, thy Lord He is mighty, merciful.

And recite to them the story of Abraham; [70] when he said to his father and his people, 'What do ye serve?' They said, 'We serve idols, and we are still devoted to them.' He said, 'Can they hear you when ye call, or profit you, or harm?'

They said, 'No; but we found our fathers doing thus.' [75] He said, 'Have ye considered what ye have been serving, ye and your fathers before you? Verily, they are foes to me, save only the Lord of the worlds, who created me and guides me, and who gives me food and drink. [80] And when I am sick He heals me; He who will kill me, and then bring me to life; and who I hope will forgive me my sins on the day of judgment! Lord, grant me judgment, and let me reach the righteous; and give me a tongue of good report amongst posterity; [85] and make me of the heirs of the paradise of pleasure; and pardon my father, verily, he is of those who err; and disgrace me not on the day when they are raised up again; the day when wealth shall profit not, nor sons, but only he who comes to God with a sound heart. [90] And paradise shall be brought near to the pious; and hell shall be brought forth to those who go astray, and it shall be said to them, "Where is what ye used to worship beside God? can they help you, or get help themselves?" And they shall fall headlong into it, they and those who have gone astray, [95] and the hosts of Iblîs all together!

'They shall say, while they quarrel therein, "By God! we were surely in an obvious error, when we made you equal to the Lord of the worlds! but it was only sinners who led us astray. [100] But we have no intercessors and no warm friend; but had we a turn we would be of the believers." '— Verily, in that is a sign, but most of them will never be believers; and, verily, thy Lord He is mighty and merciful.

[105] The people of Noah said the apostles were liars, when their brother Noah said to them, 'Will ye not fear? verily, I am a faithful apostle to you; then fear God and obey me. I do not ask you for it any hire; my hire is only with the Lord of the worlds. [110] So fear God and obey me.' They said, 'Shall we believe in thee, when the reprobates follow thee?' He said, 'I did not know what they were doing; their account is only with my Lord, if ye but perceive. And I am not one to drive away the believers, [115] I am only a plain warner.'

They said, 'Verily, if thou desist not, O Noah! thou shalt surely be of those who are stoned!' Said he, 'My Lord! verily, my people call me liar; open between me and between them an opening, and save me and those of the believers who are with me!'

So we saved him and those with him in the laden ark, [120] then we drowned the rest; verily, in that is a sign, but most of them will never be believers; and, verily, thy Lord He is mighty and merciful.

And 'Âd called the apostles liars; when their brother Hûd said to them, 'Will ye not fear? [125] Verily, I am to you a faithful apostle; then fear God and obey me. I do not ask you for it any hire; my hire is only with the Lord of the worlds. Do ye build on every height a landmark in sport, and take to works that haply ye may be immortal?

[130] 'And when ye assault ye assault like tyrants; but

fear God and obey me; and fear Him who hath given you an extent of cattle and sons, and gardens and springs. [135] Verily, I fear for you the torment of a mighty day!'

They said, 'It is the same to us if thou admonish or art not of those who do admonish; this is nothing but old folks' fictions, for we shall not be tormented!'

And they called him liar! but we destroyed them. Verily, in that is a sign, but most of them will never be believers. [140] And, verily, thy Lord is mighty, merciful.

Thamûd called the apostles liars; when their brother Zâli'h said to them, 'Do ye not fear? verily, I am to you a faithful apostle; so fear God and obey me. [145] I do not ask you for it any hire; my hire is only with the Lord of the worlds. Shall ye be left here in safety with gardens and springs, and corn-fields and palms, the spathes whereof are fine? and ye hew out of the mountains houses skilfully. [150] But fear God and obey me; and obey not the bidding of the extravagant, who do evil in the earth and do not act aright!'

They said, 'Thou art only of the infatuated; thou art but mortal like ourselves; so bring us a sign, if thou be of those who speak the truth!'

[155] He said, 'This she-camel shall have her drink and you your drink on a certain day; but touch her not with evil, or there will seize you the torment of a mighty day!'

But they hamstrung her, and on the morrow they repented; and the torment seized them; verily, in that is a sign; but most of them will never be believers: but verily, thy Lord He is mighty, merciful.

[160] The people of Lot called the apostles liars; when their brother Lot said to them, 'Do ye not fear? verily, I am to you a faithful apostle; then fear God and obey me. I do not ask you for it any hire; my hire is only with the Lord of the worlds. [165] Do ye approach males of all the world and

leave what God your Lord has created for you of your wives? nay, but ye are people who transgress!'

They said, 'Surely, if thou dost not desist, O Lot! thou shalt be of those who are expelled!'

Said he, 'Verily, I am of those who hate your deed; my Lord! save me and my people from what they do.'

[170] And we saved him and his people all together, except an old woman amongst those who lingered. Then we destroyed the others; and we rained down upon them a rain; and evil was the rain of those who were warned. Verily, in that is a sign; but most of them will never be believers. [175] And, verily, thy Lord He is mighty, merciful, compassionate.

The fellows of the Grove called the apostles liars; Sho'hâib said to them, 'Will ye not fear? verily, I am to you a faithful apostle, then fear God and obey me. [180] I do not ask you for it any hire; my hire is only with the Lord of the worlds. Give good measure, and be not of those who diminish; and weigh with a fair balance, and do not cheat men of their goods; and waste not the land, despoiling it; and fear Him who created you and the races of yore!' [185] Said they, 'Thou art only of the infatuated; and thou art only a mortal like ourselves; and, verily, we think that thou art surely of the liars; so make a portion of the heaven to fall down upon us, if thou art of those who tell the truth!'

Said he, 'My Lord knows best what ye do!' but they called him liar, and the torment of the day of the shadow seized them; for it was the torment of a mighty day: [190] verily, in that is a sign; but most of them will never be believers; but, verily, thy Lord He is mighty, merciful!

And, verily, it[1] is a revelation from the Lord of the

[1] The Qur'ân.

worlds; the Faithful Spirit came down with it[1] upon thy
heart, that thou shouldst be of those who warn;—[195] in
plain Arabic language, and, verily, it is (foretold) in the
scriptures of yore! Have they not a sign, that the learned
men of the children of Israel recognise it[2]? Had we sent it
down to any barbarian, and he had read it to them, they
would not have believed therein. [200] Thus have we made
for it[3] a way into the hearts of the sinners; they will not believe therein until they see the grievous woe! and it shall
come to them suddenly while they do not perceive! They
will say, 'Shall we be respited?—What! do they wish to hasten on our torment?'

[205] What thinkest thou? if we let them enjoy themselves for years, and then there come to them what they are
threatened, that will not avail them which they had to
enjoy! But we do not destroy any city without its having
warners as a reminder, for we are never unjust.

[210] The devils did not descend therewith; it is not fit
work for them; nor are they able to do it. Verily, they are de-
posed from listening[4]; call not then with God upon other
gods, or thou wilt be of the tormented; but warn thy clans-
men who are near of kin. [215] And lower[5] thy wing to
those of the believers who follow thee; but if they rebel
against thee, say, 'Verily, I am clear of what ye do,' and rely
thou upon the mighty, merciful One, who sees thee when
thou dost stand up, and thy posturing amongst those who
adore[6]. [220] Verily, He both hears and knows!

[1] The angel Gabriel.
[2] The Qur'ân.
[3] Infidelity.
[4] See Part I, p. 50.
[5] See Part I, p. 250, note 2.
[6] Or, it may be thy going to and fro amongst believers, as Mohammed
is reported to have done one night, to see what they were about, and he

Shall I inform you upon whom the devils descend? they descend upon every sinful liar, and impart what they have heard[1]; but most of them are liars.

And the poets do those follow who go astray! [225] Dost thou not see that they wander distraught in every vale? and that they say that which they do not do? save those who believe, and do right, and remember God much, and defend themselves after they are wronged; but those who do wrong shall know with what a turn they shall be turned[2].

---

found the whole settlement 'buzzing like a hornet's nest with the sound of the recitation of the Qur'ân and of the prayers.'

[1] That is, by listening at the door of heaven; see Part I, p. 50, note 2.

[2] That is, in what condition they shall be brought before God.

The Chapter of the Ant.

In the name of the merciful and compassionate God.

T. S. Those are the signs of the Qur'ân and the perspicuous Book; a guidance and glad tidings to the believers, who are steadfast at prayer, and give alms, and of the hereafter are sure; verily, those who believe not in the hereafter we have made seemly for them their works, and they shall wander blindly on! [5] These are they who shall have an evil torment, and they in the hereafter shall be those who most lose! Verily, thou dost meet with this Qur'ân from the wise, the knowing One!

When Moses said to his people, 'Verily, I perceive a fire, I will bring you therefrom news; or I will bring you a burning brand; haply ye may be warmed.' But when he came to it he was called to, 'Blessed be He who is in the fire, and he who is about it! and celebrated be the praises of God, the Lord of the worlds! O Moses! verily, I am God, the mighty, wise; [10] throw down thy staff!' and when he saw it quivering, as though it were a snake, he turned back fleeing, and did not return. 'O Moses! fear not; verily, as for me—apostles fear not with me; save only those who have done wrong and then substitute good for evil; for, verily, I am forgiving, merciful! but put thy hand in thy bosom, it shall come forth white without hurt;—one of nine signs to Pharaoh and his people; verily, they are a people who act abominably.'

And when our signs came to them visibly, they said, 'This is obvious sorcery!' and they gainsaid them—though their souls made sure of them—unjustly, haughtily; but, behold what was the end of the evildoers!

[15] And we gave David and Solomon knowledge; and they both said, 'Praise belongs to God, who hath preferred us over many of His servants who believe!'

And Solomon was David's heir; and said, 'O ye folk! we have been taught the speech of birds, and we have been given everything; verily, this is an obvious grace!'

And assembled for Solomon were his hosts of the ginns, and men, and birds, and they were marshalled; until they came upon the valley of the ants. Said an ant, 'O ye ants! go into your dwellings, that Solomon and his hosts crush you not while they do not perceive.'

And he smiled, laughing at her speech, and said, 'O Lord! excite me to be thankful for Thy favour, wherewith Thou hast favoured me and my parents, and to do right-eousness which may please Thee; and make me enter into Thy mercy amongst Thy righteous servants!'

[20] And he reviewed the birds, and said, 'How is it I see not the hoopoe? is he then amongst the absent? I will surely torment him with a severe torment; or I will surely slaugh-ter him; or he shall bring me obvious authority.'

And he tarried not long, and said, 'I have compassed what ye compassed not; for I bring you from Sebâ[1] a sure information: verily, I found a woman ruling over them, and she was given all things, and she had a mighty throne; and I found her and her people adoring the sun instead of God, for Satan had made seemly to them their works, and turned them from the path, so that they are not guided. [25] Will they not adore God who brings forth the secrets in the heav-ens, and knows what they hide and what they manifest?— God, there is no god but He, the Lord of the mighty throne!'

Said he, 'We will see whether thou hast told the truth, or whether thou art of those who lie. Go with this my letter

---

[1] The Sheba of the Bible, in the south of the Arabian peninsula.

and throw it before them, then turn back away from them, and see what they return.'

Said she, 'O ye chiefs! verily, a noble letter has been thrown before me. [30] It is from Solomon, and, verily, it is, "In the name of the merciful and compassionate God. Do not rise up against me, but come to me resigned!" ' She said, 'O ye chiefs! pronounce sentence for me in my affair. I never decide an affair until ye testify for me.'

They said, 'We are endowed with strength, and endowed with keen violence; but the bidding is thine, see then what it is that thou wilt bid.'

She said, 'Verily, kings when they enter a city despoil it, and make the mighty ones of its people the meanest; thus it is they do! [35] So, verily, I am going to send to them a gift, and will wait to see with what the messengers return.'

And when he came to Solomon, he said, 'Do ye proffer me wealth, when what God has given me is better than what He has given you? nay, ye in your gifts rejoice! return to them, for we will surely come to them with hosts which they cannot confront; and we will surely drive them out therefrom mean and made small!'

Said he, 'O ye chiefs! which of you will bring me her throne before they come to me resigned?'

Said a demon of the ginns, 'I will bring thee it before thou canst rise up from thy place, for I therein am strong and faithful.'

[40] He who had the knowledge of the Book[1] said, 'I will bring it to thee before thy glance can turn.' And when he saw it settled down beside him, he said, 'This is of my Lord's grace, that He may try me whether I am grateful or

---

[1] The commentators are uncertain as to whether this was 'Âzaf, Solomon's prime minister, or whether it was the prophet 'Hidhr, or the angel Gabriel, or, indeed, Solomon himself.

ungrateful, and he who is grateful is only grateful for his own soul, and he who is ungrateful,—verily, my Lord is rich and generous.'

Said he, 'Disguise for her her throne; let us see whether she is guided, or wither she is of those who are not guided.' And when she came it was said, 'Was thy throne like this?' She said, 'It might be it;' and we were given knowledge before her, but we were resigned[1].

But that which she served beside God turned her away; verily, she was of the unbelieving people. And it was said to her, 'Enter the court;' and when she saw it, she reckoned it to be an abyss of water, and she uncovered her legs. Said he, 'Verily, it is a court paved with glass!' [45] Said she, 'My Lord! verily, I have wronged myself, but I am resigned with Solomon to God the Lord of the worlds!'

And we sent unto Thamûd their brother Zâli'h, 'Serve God;' but behold, they were two parties who contended!

Said he, 'O my people! why do ye hasten on evil acts before good deeds? why do ye not ask forgiveness of God? haply ye may obtain mercy.' They said, 'We have taken an augury concerning thee and those who are with thee.' Said he, 'Your augury is in God's hands; nay, but ye are a people who are tried!'

And there were in the city nine persons who despoiled the land and did not right. [50] Said they, 'Swear to each other by God, we will surely fall on him by night and on his people; then we will surely say unto his next of kin, "We witnessed not the destruction of his people, and we do surely tell the truth!" ' And they plotted a plot, and we plotted a plot, but they did not perceive. Behold, how was the

---

[1] Commentators differ as to whether the last words are to be taken as the conclusion of the Queen of Sheba's speech, or as Solomon's comment upon it.

end of their plot, that we destroyed them and their people all together!

Thus are their houses overturned, for that they were unjust; verily, in that is a sign to people who do know!

But we saved those who believed and who did fear.

[55] And Lot when he said to his people, 'Do ye approach an abominable sin while ye can see? do ye indeed approach men lustfully rather than women? nay! ye are a people who are ignorant.' But the answer of his people was only to say, 'Drive out Lot's family from your city! verily, they are a folk who would keep pure.'

But we saved him and his family except his wife, her we destined to be of those who lingered; and we rained down upon them rain, and evil was the rain of those who were warned.

[60] Say, 'Praise belongs to God; and peace be upon His servants whom He has chosen! Is God best, or what they associate with Him?' He who created the heavens and the earth; and sends down upon you from the heaven water; and we cause to grow therewith gardens fraught with beauty; ye could not cause the trees thereof to grow! Is there a god with God? nay, but they are a people who make peers with Him! He who made the earth, settled, and placed amongst its rivers; and placed upon it firm mountains; and placed between the two seas a barrier; is there a god with God? nay, but most of them know not! He who answers the distressed when he calls upon Him and removes the evil; and makes you successors in the earth; is there a god with God? little is it that ye are mindful. He who guides you in the darkness, of the land and of the sea; and who sends winds as glad tidings before His mercy; is there a god with God? exalted be God above what they associate with Him! [65] He who began the creation and then will make it return

again; and who provides you from the heaven and the earth; is there a god with God? so bring your proofs if ye do speak the truth!

Say, 'None in the heavens or the earth know the unseen save only God; but they perceive not when they shall be raised!'—nay, but their knowledge attains to somewhat of the hereafter; nay, but they are in doubt concerning it! nay, but they are blind!

And those who disbelieved said, 'What! when we have become dust and our fathers too, shall we indeed be brought forth? [70] We were promised this, we and our fathers before us, this is nothing but old folks' tales!'

Say, 'Journey on through the land and see how was the end of the sinners! and grieve not for them, and be not straitened at what they plot.'

They say, 'When shall this threat be if ye do tell the truth?' Say, 'It may be that there is pressing close behind you a part of what ye would hasten on!' [75] But, verily, thy Lord is full of grace to men, but most of them will not be thankful; and, verily, thy Lord knows what their breasts conceal and what they manifest; and there is no secret thing in the heaven or earth, save that is in the perspicuous Book!

Verily, this Qur'ân relates to the people of Israel most of that whereon they do dispute; and, verily, it is a guidance and a mercy to the believers. [80] Verily, thy Lord decides between them by His judgment, for He decides between them by His judgment, for He is mighty, knowing. Rely thou then upon God, verily, thou art standing on obvious truth. Verily, thou canst not make the dead to hear, and thou canst not make the deaf to hear the call when they turn their backs on thee; nor art thou a guide to the blind, out of their error: thou canst only make to hear such as believe in our signs, and such as are resigned.

And when the sentence falls upon them we will bring

forth a beast out of the earth that shall speak to them, (and say) that, 'Men of our signs would not be sure.'

[85] And the day when we will gather from every nation a troop of those who said our signs were lies; and they shall be marshalled; until they come, and He will say, 'Did ye say my signs were lies, when ye had compassed no knowledge thereof? or what is it that ye were doing?' and the sentence shall fall upon them for that they did wrong, and they shall not have speech.

Did they not see that we have made the night for them to rest in, and the day to see by? verily, in that are signs to people who believe.

And the day when the trumpet shall be blown and all who are in the heavens and the earth shall be startled, save whom God pleases! and all shall come abjectly to Him. [90] And thou shalt see the mountains, which thou dost deem solid, pass away like the passing of the clouds;—the work of God who orders all things; verily, He is well aware of what ye do!

He who brings a good deed shall have better than it; and from the alarm of that day they shall be safe: but those who bring an evil deed shall be thrown down upon their faces in the fire. Shall ye be rewarded save for what ye have done?

I am bidden to serve the Lord of this country who has made it sacred, and whose are all things; and I am bidden to be of those who are resigned, and to recite the Qur'ân; and he who is guided he is only guided for himself; and he who errs,—say, 'I am only of those who warn!'

[95] And say, 'Praise be to God, He will show you His signs, and ye shall recognise them; for thy Lord is not heedless of what ye do!'

THE CHAPTER OF THE STORY.

IN the name of the merciful and compassionate God.

T. S. M. Those are the signs of the perspicuous Book; we recite to thee from the history of Moses and Pharaoh in truth unto a people who believe.

Verily, Pharaoh was lofty in the land and made the people thereof sects; one party of them he weakened, slaughtering their sons and letting their women live. Verily, he was of the despoilers.

And we wished to be gracious to those who were weakened in the earth, and to make them models, and to make them the heirs; [5] and to establish for them in the earth; and to show Pharaoh and Hâmân[1] and their hosts what they had to beware of from them.

And we inspired the mother of Moses, 'Suckle him; and when thou art afraid for him then throw him into the river, and fear not and grieve not; verily, we are going to restore him to thee, and to make him of the apostles!'

And Pharaoh's family picked him up that he might be for them a foe and a grief; verily, Pharaoh and Hâmân and their hosts were sinners.

And Pharaoh's wife said, 'He is a cheering of the eye to me, and to thee. Kill him not; it may be that he will profit us, or that we may take him for a son;' for they did not perceive.

And the heart of Moses' mother was void on the mor-

---

[1] Hâmân, according to the Qu'ârn, is made out to be the prime minister of Pharaoh.

row[1]; she well-nigh disclosed him, had it not been that we bound up her heart that she might be of the believers.

[10] And she said to his sister, 'Follow him up.' And she looked after him from afar, and they did not perceive. And we made unlawful for him the wet-nurses[2]. And she said, 'Shall I guide you to the people of the house who will take care of him for you, and who will be sincere respecting him?'

So we restored him to his mother that her eye might be cheered, and that she might not grieve, and that she might know that the promise of God is true, though most of them know not.

And when he reached puberty, and was settled, we gave him judgment and knowledge; for thus do we reward those who do well. And he entered into the city at the time the people thereof were heedless, and he found therein two men fighting; the one of his sect and the other of his foes. And he who was of his sect asked his aid against him who was of his foes; and Moses smote him with his fist and finished him. Said he, 'This is of the work of Satan, verily, he is a misleading obvious foe.'

[15] Said he, 'My Lord! verily, I have wronged my soul, but forgive me.' So He forgave him; for He is forgiving and merciful.

Said he, 'My Lord! for that Thou hast been gracious to me, I will surely not back up the sinners.'

And on the morrow he was afraid in the city, expectant. And behold, he whom he had helped the day before cried (again) to him for aid. Said Moses to him, 'Verily, thou art

---

[1] Either devoid of patience, according to some, or of anxiety, according to others, or it may be to everything but the thought of Moses.

[2] That is, Moses was made to refuse the breast of the Egyptian woman before his sister came to offer her services, and point out a nurse who would rear him.

obviously quarrelsome.' And when he wished to assault him who was the enemy to them both, he said, 'O Moses! dost thou desire to kill me as thou didst kill a person yesterday? thou dost only desire to be a tyrant in the earth; and thou dost not desire to be of those who do right!' And a man came from the remote parts of the city running, said he, 'O Moses! verily, the chiefs are deliberating concerning thee to kill thee; go then forth; verily, I am to you a sincere adviser!'

[20] So he went forth therefrom, afraid and expectant. Said he, 'Lord, save me from the unjust people!'

And when he turned his face in the direction of Midian, he said, 'It may be that my Lord will guide me to a level path!' And when he went down to the water of Midian he found thereat a nation of people watering their flocks.

And he found beside them two women keeping back their flocks. Said he, 'What is your design?' They said, 'We cannot water our flocks until the herdsmen have finished; for our father is a very old man.' So he watered for them; then he turned back towards the shade and said, 'My Lord!, verily, I stand in need of what Thou sendest down to me of good.'

[25] And one of the two came to him walking modestly; said she, 'Verily, my father calls thee, to reward thee with hire for having watered our flocks for us.' And when he came to him and related to him the story, said he, 'Fear not, thou art safe from the unjust people.' Said one of them, 'O my sire! hire him; verily, the best of those whom thou canst hire is the strong and faithful.'

Said he, 'Verily, I desire to marry thee to one of these daughters of mine, on condition that thou dost serve me for hire eight years; and if thou shalt fulfil ten it is of thyself; for I do not wish to make it wretched for thee; thou wilt find me, if it please God, of the righteous!'

Said he, 'That is between you and me; whichever of the two terms I fulfil, let there be no enmity against me, for God over what we say keeps guard.'

And when Moses had fulfilled the appointed time, and was journeying with his people, he perceived from the side of the mountain a fire; said he to his people, 'Tarry ye here; verily, I have perceived a fire, haply I may bring you good news therefrom, or a brand of fire that haply ye may be warmed.'

[30] And when he came to it he was called to, from the right side of the wady, in the blessed valley, out of the tree, 'O Moses! verily, I am God the Lord of the worlds; so throw down thy rod;' and when he saw it quivering as though it were a snake, he turned away and fled and did not return. 'O Moses! approach and fear not, verily, thou art amongst the safe. Thrust thy hand into thy bosom, it shall come out white, without hurt; and then fold again thy wing, that thou dost now stretch out through dread; for those are two signs from thy Lord to Pharaoh and his chiefs; verily, they are a people who work abomination!'

Said he, 'My Lord! verily, I have killed a person amongst them, and I fear that they will kill me: and my brother Aaron, he is more eloquent of tongue than I; send him then with me as a support, to verify me; verily, I fear that they will call me liar!'

[35] Said He, 'We will strengthen thine arm with thy brother; and we will make for you both authority, and they shall not reach you in our signs; ye two and those who follow you shall gain the upper hand.'

And when Moses came to them with our manifest signs, they said, 'This is only sorcery devised; and we have not heard of this amongst our fathers of yore.'

Moses said, 'My Lord knows best who comes with guidance from Him, and whose shall be the issue of the abode. Verily, the unjust shall not prosper!'

And Pharaoh said, 'O ye chiefs! I do not know any god for you except me; then set fire, O Hâmân! to some clay and make for me a tower, haply I may mount up to the God of Moses; for, verily, I think he is of those who lie!'

And he grew big with pride, he and his armies in the land, without right; and they thought that they to us should not return. [40] And we overtook him and his army, and we flung them into the sea; behold, then, how was the end of the unjust.

But we made them models calling to the fire; and on the resurrection day they shall not be helped; and we followed them up in this world with a curse; and on the resurrection day they shall be abhorred!

And we gave Moses the Book, after that we had destroyed the former generations, as an insight to men and a guidance and a mercy; haply they may be mindful!

Thou wast not upon the western side when we decided for Moses, but afar off; nor wast thou of the witnesses. [45] But we raised up (other) generations, and life was prolonged for them; and thou wast not staying admist the people of Midian, reciting to them our signs; but we were sending our apostles.

Nor wast thou by the side of the mountain when we called; but it is a mercy from thy Lord, that thou mayest warn a people to whom no warner has come before thee; haply they may be mindful! And lest there should befall them a mishap for what their hands have sent before, and they should say, 'Our Lord! why didst thou not send to us an apostle? for we would have followed thy signs and been of the believers.'

And when the truth comes to them from us they say, 'We

are given the like of what Moses was given.' Did they not disbelieve in what Moses was given before?—they say, 'Two works of sorcery[1] back up each other;' and they say, 'Verily, we do disbelieve in all.'

Say, 'Bring, then, a book from God which shall be a better guide than both, and I will follow it, if ye do tell the truth!'

[50] And if they cannot answer thee, then know that they follow their own lusts; and who is more in error than he who follows his own lust without guidance from God? verily, God guides not an unjust people!

And we caused the word to reach them, haply they may be mindful!

Those to whom we gave the Book before it, they believe therein; and when it is recited to them they say, 'We believe in it as truth from our Lord; verily, we were resigned before it came!' These shall be given their hire twice over, for that they were patient, and repelled evil with good, and of what we have bestowed upon them give alms.

[55] And when they hear vain talk, they turn away from it and say, 'We have our works, and ye have your works. Peace be upon you! we do not seek the ignorant!'

Verily, thou canst not guide whom thou dost like, but God guides whom He pleases; for He knows best who are to be guided.

And they say, 'If we follow the guidance we shall be snatched away from the land.' Have we not established for them a safe sanctuary, to which are imported the fruits of everything as a provision from us? but most of them do not know.

How many a city have we destroyed that exulted in its means of subsistence? These are their dwellings, never dwelt in after them, except a little; for we were the heirs.

---

[1] That is, the Pentateuch and Qu'ârn.

But thy Lord would never destroy cities until He sent to the metropolis thereof an apostle, to recite to them our signs; nor would we destroy cities unless their people were unjust. [60] Whatever thing ye may be given, it is a provision for this world's life and the adornment thereof; but what is with God is better and more enduring; have ye then no sense?

Is He to whom we have promised a goodly promise, which he shall meet with, like him to whom we have given the enjoyment of the life of this world, and who upon the resurrection day shall be of the arraigned?

And on the day when He will call them and will say, 'Where are those associates which ye did pretend?' And those against whom the sentence is due shall say, 'Our Lord! these are those whom we have seduced; we seduced them as we were seduced ourselves: but we clear ourselves to thee;—they did not worship us!'

And it will be said, 'Call upon your partners;' and they will call upon them, but they will not answer them, and they shall see the torment; would that they had been guided.

[65] And the day when He shall call them and shall say, 'What was it ye answered the apostles?' and the history shall be blindly confusing to them on that day, and they shall not ask each other.

But, as for him who turns again and believes and does right, it may be that he will be among the prosperous. For thy Lord creates what He pleases and chooses; they have not the choice! Celebrated be the praise of God! and exalted be He above what they associate with Him!

Thy Lord knows what they conceal in their breasts and what they manifest.

[70] He is God, there is no god but He; to Him belongs praise, in the first and the last; and His is the judgment; and unto Him shall ye return!

Have ye considered, if God were to make for you the night endless until the resurrection day, who is the god, but God, to bring you light? can ye not then hear?

Say, 'Have ye considered, if God were to make for you the day endless until the day of judgment, who is the god, except God, to bring you the night to rest therein? can ye not then see?' But of His mercy He has made for you the night and the day, that ye may rest therein, and crave of His grace, haply ye may give thanks.

And the day when He shall call them and shall say, 'Where are my partners whom ye did pretend?' [75] And we will pluck from every nation a witness; and we will say, 'Bring your proof and know that the truth is God's;' and that which they had devised shall stray away from them.

Verily, Korah[1] was of the people of Moses, and he was outrageous against them; and we gave him treasuries of which the keys would bear down a band of men endowed with strength. When his people said to him, 'Exult not; verily, God loves not those who exult! but crave, though what God has given thee, the future abode; and forget not thy portion in this world, and do good, as God has done good to thee; and seek not evil doing in the earth; verily, God loves not the evildoers!'

Said he, 'I have only been given it for knowledge which I have!' did he not know that God had destroyed before him many generations of those who were stronger than he, and had amassed more? But the sinners need not to be asked concerning their crimes.

And he went out amongst the people in his ornaments; those who desired the life of this world said, 'O would that

---

[1] In Arabic Qârûn. The legend based upon Talmudic tradition of Korah's immense wealth appears to be also confused with that of Crœsus.

we had the like of what Korah had been given! verily, he is endowed with mighty fortune!'

[80] But those who had been given knowledge said, 'Woe to you! the reward of God is better for him who believes and does right; but none shall meet with it except the patient. And we clave the earth with him and with his house; and he had no troop to help him against God, nor was he of those who were helped!'

And on the morrow those who had yearned for his place the day before said, 'Ah, ah! God extends provisions to whom He pleases of His servants, or He doles it out; had not God been gracious to us, the earth would have cleft open with us! Ah, ah! the unbelievers shall not prosper!'

That is the future abode; we make it for those who do not wish to be haughty in the earth, nor to do evil, and the end is for the pious.

He who brings a good deed shall have better than it; and he who brings an evil deed—those who do evil deeds shall only be rewarded for that which they have done. [85] Verily, He who hath ordained the Qu'ârn for thee will restore thee to thy returning place. Say, 'My Lord knows best who brings guidance, and who is in obvious error; nor couldst thou hope that the Book would be thrown to thee, save as a mercy from thy Lord! be not then a backer up of those who misbelieve; and let them not turn thee from the signs of God, after they have been sent down to thee; but call unto thy Lord and be not of the idolaters; and call not with God upon any other god; there is no god but He! everything is perishable, except His face; His is the judgment, and unto Him shall ye return!